"No husband wants to be in the] if that's you, be assured that the guidance you'll receive in this book is the rare kind, characterized by both confidence in the power of Jesus Christ and the humility that comes only from acknowledging personal weakness."

Jeremy Pierre, Lawrence and Charlotte Hoover Professor of Biblical Counseling & Department Chair, The Southern Baptist Theological Seminary; author of *The Dynamic Heart in Daily Life* and *When Home Hurts*

"*Redeem Your Marriage* is a helpful guide for both husbands struggling with porn and those who are helping other men. Curtis offers sound, biblical, and practical understanding of this struggle while showing how the corresponding heart dynamics impact every aspect of our lives. In addition, he shows how affection for Christ is the ultimate pathway forward. I recommend this resource for both church members and leaders alike."

Robert K. Cheong, Pastor of Care, Sojourn Church Midtown; executive director, Gospel Care Ministries; author of *Restoration Story* and *Restore*

"This is one of the most important books any married couple will read. Take in these truths and let them encourage you, strengthen you, and challenge you to fight for what matters most: each other."

Chad M. Robichaux, Founder, Mighty Oaks Foundation

"Curtis and Jenny Solomon's books, written as husband and wife to husbands and wives in the throes of pornography's sobering devastation, provide gentle yet sinewy and personal encouragement and guidance. Reading these books felt like sitting with trustworthy companions for couples who need Christ's courage and hope regarding repentance and freedom from porn and the pain it brings to marriages."

Ellen Mary Dykas, Director of Women's Ministry, Harvest USA; author of *Sexual Sanity for Women* and *Toxic Relationships*; coauthor of *Sexual Faithfulness*

"There are many helpful books out there for men struggling with pornography. What makes this book unique is its focus on what repentance looks like in the context of marriage. This book and its companion volume for wives will be my go-to resource for husbands and wives looking to honor God and grow together as they seek to rebuild a strong marriage damaged by porn use."

Nathanael Brooks, Assistant Professor of Christian Counseling, Reformed Theological Seminary, Charlotte, NC

"Curtis and Jenny have much wisdom to share with couples who are hurting as a result of one partner's use of porn. I would encourage couples to learn from them how to glorify Jesus in the midst of great hurt."

Amy Baker, Ministry Resource Director at Faith Church, Lafayette, IN; author of *Getting to the Heart of Friendships* and *Picture Perfect*; editor of *Caring for the Souls of Children*

"*Redeem Your Marriage* is refreshingly honest and compassionate about the difficulty of the sexual struggles men face. It's honest about how heavily porn impacts wives, as well as both the challenge and the real possibility of genuine and lasting change. Best of all, it comes from an author brave enough to be honest about his own struggle! I highly recommend it!"

Alasdair Groves, Executive Director of the Christian Counseling and Educational Foundation (CCEF); coauthor of *Untangling Emotions*

"When I teach on human sexuality and its many perversions, you'd think that students would cringe and clam up. Such is not the case, however. The biggest difficulty is knowing how to start the discussion. Curtis Solomon's book, *Redeem Your Marriage*, has been forged out of brokenness and is filled with gracious counsel. It's the ideal starting point for difficult discussions."

Gregg R. Allison, Professor of Christian Theology, The Southern Baptist Theological Seminary; secretary, Evangelical Theological Society; author of *Embodied: Living as Whole People in a Fractured World*

"The truth is that we all live in a terribly broken world, where men who should protect and care for their sisters instead use and abuse them for their own selfish pleasure. My brother, Curtis Solomon, knows about this brokenness—he knows about it personally and he knows about it as a man who wants to help others find freedom, health, and holiness. Curtis's willingness to put himself out there in humility and to fight for holiness is breathtaking and I'm personally so proud to call him my brother. And I'm so thankful for this book. You will be too."

Elyse Fitzpatrick, Coauthor of *Worthy: Celebrating the Value of Women*

"I am certain that this new pair of books by my friends Curtis and Jenny Solomon will serve many couples as they redeem and reclaim a marriage that has been harmed by pornography. Those who read these books will find them helpful, challenging, encouraging, and best of all, biblical."

Tim Challies, Blogger at Challies.com; author of *Epic: An Around-the-World Journey through Christian History*

Redeem
Your Marriage

Hope for Husbands Who Have Hurt
through Pornography

Curtis Solomon

New
Growth
Press

newgrowthpress.com

New Growth Press, Greensboro, NC 27401
newgrowthpress.com

Cover Design: Faceout Books, faceoutstudios.com
Interior Typesetting: Lisa Parnell, lparnellbookservices.com

ISBN: 978-1-64507-225-6 (Print)

ISBN: 978-1-64507-226-3 (eBook)

Library of Congress Cataloging-in-Publication Data
Names: Solomon, Curtis, author.
Title: Redeem your marriage : hope for husbands who have hurt through
pornography / Curtis Solomon.
Description: Greensboro, NC : New Growth Press, [2022] | Includes
bibliographical references and index. | Summary: "As a husband, what can
you do when you are caught in the prison of pornography use? It might
be tempting to give up and give in, but there is hope for your struggle and
there is hope for your marriage"— Provided by publisher.
Identifiers: LCCN 2021046193 (print) | LCCN 2021046194 (ebook) | ISBN
9781645072256 (print) | ISBN 9781645072263 (ebook)
Subjects: LCSH: Marriage—Religious aspects—Christianity. | Husbands—
Religious life. | Pornography—Religious aspects—Christianity.
Classification: LCC BV835 .S745 2022 (print) | LCC BV835 (ebook) | DDC
248.8/44—dc23
LC record available at https://lccn.loc.gov/2021046193
LC ebook record available at https://lccn.loc.gov/2021046194

Printed in the United States of America

29 28 27 26 25 24 23 22   1 2 3 4 5

DEDICATION

For Jenny

Contents

Foreword ix

Acknowledgments xi

Introduction 1

1. Fallen Leaves 7

2. Lament 16

3. Repentance 25

4. The Fruits of Repentance 39

5. Forgiveness 52

6. Admiration: Worshiping Jesus 65

7. Accountability 72

8. Your Wife Is Your Second Greatest Ally 83

9. Amputations and Alterations 96

10. Living Like David 115

Appendices

1. Porn and Abuse 119

2. Ministry after Porn 125

3. Is Pornography Use Grounds for Divorce? 141

Endnotes 146

Foreword

WHAT YOU ARE about to read will be so helpful for your marriage. If pornography has invaded your heart and, as a result, your relationship, you might think that the way to reconciliation is a lonely one. That is, you believe you must work on your problem by yourself until it is behind you, *then* you can work on your marriage. This book will take you on a different path—it will help you do this work together.

Together is more unusual than you might think. You hope to help her, encourage her, and bless her, but you are the author of her misery. This, it would seem, disqualifies you from even trying to care for her, or from *ever* trying to care for her. You would naturally think it best to distance yourself: the further away you are, the better she is. Instead, this book will take you on a more hopeful course.

You should know a few things about Curtis. A skilled guide has been there before you. He knows the best routes and the places that are most dangerous. Having tripped up in some of those places, he is gentle with others who fall. This is what you will receive from him. He knows that this work might be the hardest you have ever done. At those times, he comes alongside you and speaks a word of encouragement. Then he will give you one small step that seems good and doable, and you keep going.

He is open, even transparent—and that will inspire you. Doesn't a book like this have more credibility when you know that the author's wife has read every word? Curtis and Jenny have discussed this together. They have wept together and grown together. She has even written a book for wives. Everything you read here has been selected because it has proved to be important in their relationship. You will notice an occasional reference to the military, in which Curtis served, and it offers another way to say this. If you are under the authority of a drill sergeant and you are beginning to tire of the harsh routine, you respond according to the sergeant's experience. If he has never been off the military base, you wonder why all the drills are necessary. But if he is a decorated veteran who has seen both death and victory and he has selected every drill because of his desire for you to know life and not death, you listen to every word.

Curtis brings many skills that will serve you. Most important is this: when you are overwhelmed and everything good seems to be removed from your life, you hear Jesus, who says, "whoever comes to me I will never cast out" (John 6:37).

Edward T. Welch
Author, speaker, biblical counselor

Acknowledgments

WITHOUT THE PEOPLE mentioned here, and others, I would not and could not have written this book.

For starters, I did not want to write this book. It wasn't my idea, this isn't a topic I've ever wanted to address, and the fact that it required sharing my own personal struggles made it even less desirable. So I must thank those who encouraged me to write the book you are holding. I say encouraged, knowing the etymology means to give courage. Without these people I would not have had the courage it took to put these words in print. Barbara Juliani, who encouraged me both by asking me to consider a book that would accompany my wife's brilliant work, and by setting an example allowing one's story to be used by God. Andy Crouch, whom I've never met, encouraged me through his book *Strong and Weak* (read it and you will know how). David Powlison, my dear friend, whose parting charge to the graduating class at Westminster Seminary in 2019 encouraged me to lead with public weakness. And of course, Jenny and Jesus, but more on them later. Without these people, I would not have written this book.

The following group of people made it possible to write once I had the courage to do so. The whole New Growth team, specifically those who helped edit the multiple drafts—Sarah, Ruth, and Irene. Thank you for making my writing comprehensible and conform to some standard of the English language. Audra and Cheryl, thank you for helping us get the word out about these books.

To those who advised and helped address the questions of abuse as it relates to pornography, your insights are invaluable and the content you shared is worth the price of admission: Darby Strickland, Kïrsten Christianson, Joy Forest, Ann Maree Goudz-waard, Jeremy Pierre, Greg Wilson, and Chris Moles. Thank you all for the tremendously difficult work you do.

Of course, I could not and would not have written this book without my wonderful wife Jenny. Your courage, bravery, humil-ity, sacrifice, and forgiveness are inspiring. I love you more today than I did yesterday.

Most of all I must thank my Lord, Savior, and Sanctifier Jesus. This is his story, not mine.

Introduction

I DID NOT grow up in a wealthy home. I never went hungry, but there were times when we had to rely on means of provision that wealthy people never imagine for themselves. With a dad who worked construction in the 1980s, we sometimes lived on unemployment and even government assistance. I didn't know it until much later in life, but at times my dad sold prized possessions, like his .44 magnum, to provide for his family. I don't know whether you've ever been to a pawnshop or what you think of them. They certainly can serve a beneficial purpose. People who need money and can't get work but have valuable items can utilize a pawnshop to provide for their needs. There is also the hope—at least for a time—that they can buy back the item they pawned. The act of purchasing back your pawned item is to redeem it.

Pawnshops also have some dark realities. For one thing, the owners of a pawnshop can take advantage of people in several ways. They can offer a person a miniscule percentage of the value of the item being pawned. For instance, they might offer less than $100 for a gun that is worth almost $1,000. The person pawning his item is, in one sense, being cheated on the front end of the deal. Pawnshop owners can also cheat the person on the back end of the deal by charging an exorbitant fee to allow him to repurchase the pawned item. In our example, they might charge that same man $500 to get his gun back only one month later. Another dark reality associated with pawnshops is that sometimes people who utilize them are exchanging valuable heirlooms so that they can purchase wasteful items to satisfy temporary desires.

Can you imagine taking your wife's engagement ring down to a pawnshop, selling it for $20, and spending the money on a meal at McDonald's? Ludicrous, right? But if you are reading this book for yourself, then you have done something far more foolish. You have taken something very precious and pawned it away, not for something far less valuable but for something gross and destructive. You have taken your marriage, the trust that was given to you, the beautiful gift of a sexually exclusive union, and pawned it for cheap thrills that promised a good time but left you craving more and enslaved you to their power.

I don't know what you are feeling as you read these words. You may be getting frustrated and defensive, or you may be feeling overwhelmed by shame and guilt. I pray you are feeling something, and I pray those feelings lead to change. I know of a pastor who once confronted a church because they were harboring gross sexual sin in the congregation. They were even patting themselves on the back for being loving and tolerant of the sexual sin that was taking place in the church. When the pastor rebuked them, it made them feel horrible. They were greatly saddened by their sin, and that sorrow led them to change the way they were living and address the sin in their midst. The church standing up for purity led those living in sexual sin to change their ways. That pastor was the apostle Paul, and he recounts that experience in 2 Corinthians 7:8–12. He was thankful that he caused them sorrow if it was truly godly sorrow. That kind of sorrow leads to change and life. If, however, it had only generated "worldly sorrow" he would have grieved because that kind of sorrow does not result in change, but leads to death. I pray that whatever you feel, it is of God and it draws you closer to him through this process. I am not writing this in condemnation over you, but as a fellow sinner. I have been there, standing at the counter, handing over the invaluable heart of my beloved for a few bucks to spend on my own pleasures. I've gone back to the shop, hoping to buy back what I've sold, only to realize I could never afford to get it back on my own. And I've been back to that same shop with even more valuables, time and time again.

I am not writing this book merely to commiserate and encourage you with the knowledge that you are not alone; I'm writing to offer you hope—hope that is not based on your ability to buy back what you have sold. Instead, the hope you will read about in these pages is the hope that One has stepped in to redeem what you could not redeem for yourself. In Christ our great Redeemer, there is hope that your heart and your marriage can be redeemed.

If you are reading this book, I am sorry; but I am also thankful. I am sorry because it likely means that you have hurt your wife, or someone you know has hurt his wife by using pornography. I am thankful because there is hope in these pages for the husband who has hurt and the wife who has been hurt. While I refer to the husband as the one who has used pornography and the wife as the one who has been hurt, I don't mean to give the impression that women do not use pornography; I know that pornography is a huge problem for women as well. However, the majority of porn users are men, and in the majority of Christian marriages that have been harmed by porn, the husband is the primary user. Therefore, the terminology used will focus on husbands, but if you are a woman who has hurt your marriage with porn, there are also valuable lessons for you here. Don't feel like you are somehow worse than other women or alone in your struggle; you are not. Wherever you are, keep reading. Keep growing toward Christ.

There are enough books on fighting pornography to keep you reading for years to come, and I'll recommend that you read some of them in addition to this one. At the end of the chapters, I will also recommend further resources related to the chapter's content if you want to learn more about a particular topic. Some of the content will overlap because the biblical principles that lead to transformation do not change. This book is distinctive because it is written in tandem with my wife's book, *Reclaim Your Marriage: Grace for Wives Who Have Been Hurt by Pornography*. As I mentioned above, I'm writing this book out of my own struggle with pornography. We wanted to bring wisdom, hope, and healing to other couples who are fighting the battles we have fought and continue to fight. Additionally, I have been a biblical counselor now for more than two decades. I have ministered in churches, parachurch ministries, and academic settings and have cared for people who struggle with pornography in all of them. What I share in this book is a compilation of what I have learned from the Lord through his word, my own struggle, and my experience counseling others. Meanwhile, Jenny's book will meet your wife where she likely is at the moment—in a place of hurt, frustration, and vulnerability—and point to God's grace for her suffering and her hope in Christ.

These books can be used alone or walked through together as a couple. The absolute best context for using them will be in relationship with another godly, wise couple who love you and are willing to walk this journey with you. It can be a pastor and his wife, a pair of biblical counselors (biblical counselors can be full-time vocational counselors or people in your church who have been trained to apply God's Word to life's problems and volunteer their time), your small group leaders, or godly friends you trust and respect. One of the principles we discuss in the books is the need to have others in your life who know you and your struggle and can be sources of wisdom and hope as you grow. Isolation will only breed further failure and frustration. If you picked this book up on your own, then I encourage you to pick up the phone and call a trusted spiritual mentor—right now—to ask him to go through it with you.

My primary motivation for writing this book is from love for Jesus. While I certainly want you to be helped, and I will share hope from my own experience, it all comes down to Christ. His glory is our central motivation for growth and change; his grace is what we need to overcome the shame and guilt brought by our porn use; his power will enable you to overcome; his grace will catch you if you fail again; and his love will hold you fast to himself. This book is all about Jesus. I pray it helps you draw closer to him. Consider these words of God, expressed by the apostle Paul in Titus 2:11–14:

> For the grace of God has appeared, bringing salvation for all people, training us to renounce ungodliness and worldly passions, and to live self-controlled, upright, and godly lives in the present age, waiting for our blessed hope, the appearing of the glory of our great God and Savior Jesus Christ, who gave himself for us to redeem us from all lawlessness and to purify for himself a people for his own possession who are zealous for good works.

This verse encapsulates so much of what I want to pass along to you and what has been central to my heart as I wrote this book. I pray that it inspires you to fight for your marriage and informs you how to do so. This book is not a program to completely abolish your desire for porn. There are no boxes you can check, no steps you can take, that will eradicate sexual lust from your heart and guarantee that you will never again look at porn. By God's grace, this book will be a help to you. It will teach you about the seriousness of pornography and encourage you to lament your sin and the losses you've suffered in life. It will walk you through the process of repentance, forgiveness, and reconciliation. And it will encourage you to find allies to help you in the fight against pornography and for the redemption of your marriage.

Your greatest ally of all is Jesus Christ himself. True transformation in weeding the pornography out of your life is first and foremost about your ongoing, growing relationship with him. Regardless of how you feel, if you love Jesus, then he is for you, not against you. He is your advocate, friend, brother, and ally in this fight (1 John 2:1, Romans 8:16–17, John 15:12–17). You may have gotten yourself into a messy, hard, difficult situation, but you cannot climb out of it on your own—you can only climb out with the help of others. To God be the glory for great things he has done—and will do in you.

1

Fallen Leaves

BECAUSE I GREW up in the desert, I was unfamiliar with the labor of raking fall leaves. After we moved to Kentucky and purchased a home with a yard full of trees, I was inducted into this annual chore. The first year we were here I was still completing my doctorate, so we hired a leaf removal company to do the job. It was far more expensive than we had anticipated so I promised my wife that I would save money by doing it myself the next year. The year flew by, but writing the dissertation did not. However, wanting to keep my word and our money, I set about picking up all those leaves. It seems there are a couple of strategies to this work (although I'm still no expert). The first strategy is to pick up the leaves progressively as they fall; the second strategy is to wait until they are all off the trees and then dispose of them in one fell swoop. For numerous reasons, I chose the progressive cleanup option. So for several weeks in a row, I spent multiple evenings after work raking, mulching, and bagging leaves. In addition, I spent the majority of my days off doing this laborious task. It was a mountain of work! After the last of the leaves were off the trees and gathered into bags, I rejoiced—no more of that until next year! Or so I thought.

The week after I had bagged the final leaves from our trees, I noticed an accumulation of new leaves, primarily along one side of our yard. I examined our trees to be sure I had not overlooked some new, late falling leaves or some other explanation for where these leaves had come from. The examination did not reveal any oversight on my part. However, it did reveal the source of the leaves. These new leaves had a strange similarity to the multitude of leaves blanketing my neighbor's yard. Mildly irritated, I gathered the leaves, mulched them, put them into cans, and set them out to be collected. All the while, I assumed this would be the last time I'd have to touch leaves that year.

My assumption turned out to be false. The next week the leaves were back. What in the world happened? Out came the leaf collection paraphernalia, and this time with slightly more irritation, I dealt with the leaves. Trying to believe the best, I assumed that the oversight was due to the fact that the neighbors were new to this kind of work; after all, they had just moved in during the summer. *Surely they will get to the leaves this week*, I thought.

Week after week for the next month, my days off were consumed by dealing with my neighbor's leaves. I could feel the irritation growing and my blood pressure soaring to new heights. *How could they? Don't they realize how hard I have worked over these past months? Haven't they seen me out here night after night, weekend after weekend, striving to keep this yard clean? And what have they been doing this whole time? They have been neglecting their responsibilities and making a mess for everyone else to clean up—how unfair!*

Unfair indeed! Like my neighbor's leaves blowing into my yard, the consequences of using pornography spill over into the lives of those around the one using it. However, unlike my fiascoes with the leaves, the effects of pornography use are deeply serious and potentially life-altering. Every one of us faces sexual temptation. We are all called to flee temptation and pursue righteousness. Those who experience victory over sexual temptation do so with the ongoing help of God's Spirit. Meanwhile, those who do not fight for purity are like my neighbor; they allow the dead leaves—representing the consequences of their sin—to pile up in the yard and spill out. The results cannot be contained by invisible boundary lines. Everyone in close relationship with pornography users will be affected by the consequences of this sin.

The Truth Will Set You Free

If you are reading this book, you have probably already begun to see this reality. You have begun to see the effects of your sin on your wife. I want to grow your understanding of these impacts. My motivation is not to condemn you, but to deepen and broaden your understanding of the insidious nature of pornography so that you will be even more committed to fight against it. The truth is always valuable. Knowing about pornography, where it comes from, the lives impacted by it, and how its use infects each of your relationships can be great fuel to stoke the fire of your hatred for your sin and your desire to live for Jesus and him alone.

We tell ourselves many lies to justify pornography—and the culture reinforces them. Some of these lies include:

- "Everyone does it."
- "I'm not hurting anyone; it's just a private thing."
- "I don't do it as much, or to the same degree, as those guys."
- "My wife is okay with it."
- "It's not as bad as adultery."

These are just a few things we might say (or think) to excuse, justify, downplay, or make ourselves comfortable with our sin. But these statements are lies; they do not align with the truth. The remainder of this chapter will counter these lies by describing the true nature of pornography. My hope and prayer is that you will begin to lose your appetite for it and to develop a hunger and thirst for righteousness (Matthew 5:6).

Is Pornography a Victimless Sin?

It may seem like your pornography use is an issue between you and God and no one else. However, when you view pornography in any form, there were likely numerous people involved in its creation. At a minimum, it involved the person or people portrayed in the pornographic images and the people creating the images. If it was professionally made, there was a whole team of producers, directors, technical operators, support staff, makeup artists, editors, etc. involved. Then there are the people responsible for hosting, delivering, and distributing the pornography. Even "amateur" porn enlists at least a handful of other people before it gets to your eyeballs.

Many women who participate in the adult entertainment industry wish they could get out of that work, and some are sex slaves who have been robbed of their freedom, held against their will, and forced to perform indecent acts so that men like us can gratify selfish desires with momentary, poisoned pleasure. Your participation fuels an industry that fosters human trafficking.[1]

Not only does your porn use support an industry that exploits and objectifies women, every relationship you have has been or is being affected by it because pornography changes you.[2] Viewing pornography changes the way you see people, especially women. Even your close male friends are affected. Unless they are helping you overcome your sin, or they are complicit in your sexual deviancy, they are deceived about who you really are.

If you have children, they will be influenced by your behavior, including your deceptions, mood alterations that occur due to porn use, and legacy you leave for them to follow. One study listed the following negative effects that children of pornography users may face:

- Encountering pornographic material a parent has acquired
- Encountering a parent masturbating

- Overhearing a parent engaged in phone sex
- Witnessing and experiencing stress in the home caused by online sexual activities
- Having increased risk of becoming consumers of pornography themselves
- Witnessing and being involved in parental conflict
- Being exposed to the commodification of human beings, especially women, as "sex objects"
- Having increased risk of parental job loss and financial strain
- Having increased risk of parental separation and divorce
- Experiencing decreased parental time and attention—both from the pornography addicted parent and from the parent preoccupied with the addicted spouse.[3]

In addition to these effects, many children will lose out on loving, active parental guidance related to sexuality because fathers who are engaged in pornography use often avoid the topic with their children. Many dads feel hypocritical about addressing sexuality because of their struggle with pornography. Others might not see it as significant, because pornography use has a tendency to diminish sensitivity to sexual sin and sexually deviant behavior.[4]

On the flip side, some fathers become hyper controlling toward their children out of fear that they may fall into similar sinful patterns, or become victims of sexual crime due to the rampant sexualization in our culture. There are likely many other ways children are negatively impacted by their parent's porn use, but these possibilities strongly illustrate the point that porn affects this relationship.

Since you are married, the life most devastated by your sin is the life of the person you promised to love, honor, cherish, and be faithful to for as long as you both live. You could be in a number of different situations right now when it comes to your wife's knowledge of your struggle:

- She may be unaware of your porn use.
- She may be reeling in the aftermath of learning about your porn use for the first time.
- She may be reeling with the latest revelation in a long line of disclosures or discoveries.
- She may be in the dark about your most recent use(s) of porn, thinking this sin was dealt with long ago when, in reality, it has just been covered by your deception yet again.

Regardless of how much your wife knows, your sin has hurt her. You have been dishonest, violated her trust, broken promises to her, demonstrated discontent with her, and directed your sexual desires and energy toward other women. If she does know, you have incited in her temptation for fear, doubt, anxiety, discontent with her own body, suspicion of other women, etc. She will most likely feel some combination of betrayed, exploited, confused, angry, sad, and alone. I hope this grieves your heart. Again, I do not want to heap shame on you; my desire is that it will bring you to a godly sorrow that leads to repentance (2 Corinthians 7:8–10).

Part of the reason your wife is so affected by your sin is that, at its core, sinful sexual lust is heart adultery. Jesus makes this point clear when he raises the stakes on lustful glances in Matthew 5:28, saying, "everyone who looks at a woman with lustful intent has already committed adultery with her in his heart." He is contrasting this idea with the clear ordinance given in the Ten Commandments: "You shall not commit adultery" (Exodus 20:14). His contrast is not intended to diminish the command given by God, but to broaden our understanding of the nature of sin. It is not merely the external act of sex outside of marriage that God abhors—it is the heart inclined in that direction as well. Wives reeling in the aftermath of a disclosure or discovery of pornography use will have a similar experience to those who find out that their spouse has committed adultery. All the who, what, when, how, and why questions will spin in her mind. She will feel betrayed, rejected, used, forsaken, and unloved. Satan will try to use your sin to plant seeds of fear, anger, doubt, and bitterness in her heart, all aimed to divide her from you and from her Savior (Ephesians 4:26–27).

The most significant person you have sinned against makes your sin far worse than you can fathom. The Bible teaches us that when we sin, no matter who else is harmed or hurt, our sin is first and foremost against God. In King David's famous song of penitence, Psalm 51, this man who sexually violated a woman and then murdered her husband to cover up his sin exclaims to God, "Against you, you only, have I sinned." David is not downplaying his clear sins against Bathsheba (rape and the subsequent murder of her husband; 2 Samuel 11). David is not ignoring the sins of betrayal, deception, and murder he committed against Uriah. Nor does this proclamation neglect the countless other people that David's sin touched: his other wives, his children, the servants involved in summoning Bathsheba, or the soldiers implicated in the murder of Uriah. What David is acknowledging is that his sin against God is so much greater than all these other sins that they fade into obscurity when compared to the vast heinousness of sinning against a perfect, all-loving God. David had sinned against his loving Creator who had brought him into being and was sustaining his very existence each and every moment.

Every sin is an attack against the God of the universe. Here is just a smattering of the ways that your pornography use is a sin committed against our perfect God:

1. You have violated his mandate for sexual purity by lusting after women who are not your wife.

2. You have demonstrated discontentment with his gracious gift of sex in the context of marriage and discontentment with the wife that God has given you.

3. You have supplanted God as the supreme ruler of your life and enthroned yourself in his place.

4. You have treated his daughters as objects to satisfy your selfish desires, rather than as the image bearers of God that they are.

5. You have misused his creative gifts by using the technologies invented by humans for evil purposes, rather than God-glorifying ones.

6. You have used your mind and body, which were designed and given to you by God, as instruments for committing shameful deeds.

7. If you are a believer in Jesus Christ, you have defiled the temple of the Holy Spirit (1 Corinthians 6:18–19).

8. You have wasted the precious and limited gift of time for illicit, self-centered pursuits when you could have been pursuing Christ and his glory.

The list could go on and on and will be slightly different for each person. Regardless of which specific ways you have sinned against God in your porn use, each lustful thought or action is far worse in scope and severity than you imagine. Every aspect of your heart—thoughts, desires, and motivations—is involved. Your whole being, body and soul, takes part in this sin. Each single act of porn use entails committing many sins against God.

This reality is painful, but that pain is not necessarily bad. Dealt with the wrong way, it can be devastating. Handled the right way, this pain can be fuel for lasting transformation. My goal is not to leave you in despair, beaten down by this knowledge. My goal, first and foremost, is to point you to Christ. I want you to despair over your sin, but I don't want to leave you there. I want you to see your sin for what it is, but then I want you to turn your gaze upward toward Christ, allow him to pull you out of the muck, and walk with him through the rest of eternity. The path forward with Christ is full of muddy pits that you will stumble or dive into from time to time, but Christ will never leave you. He will be there with you to pick you out of the mire, clean you off, comfort you, and encourage you to press on in the journey.

In the next chapter, we will examine the process of moving upward and onward from the depth of your sin to the heights of a life that reflects Christ. For now, take some time to prayerfully reflect on your sin, the consequences it has inflicted on others, and how it has separated you from them and your creator.

Questions for Action, Discussion, and Reflection

1. How do the realities presented in this chapter impact your understanding of your use of pornography? How do they impact you emotionally? How do they influence your desires for your life moving forward?

2. Who have you sinned against directly or indirectly with your use of pornography? How have they been affected?

3. What are some ways your sin has been a direct affront to God (you can use the list from this chapter or add others)? Spend time acknowledging this to him, and ask him to help you understand these realities more deeply.

Further Reading on Fighting Pornography and Sexual Sin

Lambert, Heath. *Finally Free: Fighting for Purity with the Power of Grace*. Grand Rapids: Zondervan, 2013.

Reju, Deepak. *Pornography: Fighting for Purity*. 31-Day Devotionals for Life. Phillipsburg, New Jersey: P&R Publishing, 2018.

2

Lament

I DON'T KNOW about you, but when I was in junior high, I was a bit of a pyromaniac. It seems like there is a budding pyro in many of us around that age. Thankfully, most of us grow out of it and don't end up doing major damage with the fire that fascinates us. One of the things that doused the flame of my pyromania was the time my friends and I almost caught a whole mountain range on fire.

My buddies and I had become quite adept (at least in our own minds) at taking apart various combustible materials, rearranging their configuration, and deploying them as some type of flammable and/or explosive device (details intentionally left vague for the protection of us all). On one particular day, we hiked out into the desert mountains behind a friend's house to set off some of these devices. After setting off a few smaller ones, we pulled out the BIG ONE and lit the fuse. We all ran for cover behind various rocks and boulders and awaited the bang. We cheered and shouted with excitement as the loud blast rocked our ears and sent bits of flaming material all around. Our excitement quickly turned to horror as those bits of flaming shrapnel landed in the dry desert vegetation. The excellent kindling provided by these sun-baked bushes caught fire and quickly became engulfed in flame. Thankfully, we all sprang into action and began stamping out the flames. We were aided by the fact that the terrain was rocky and the vegetation sparse so that the flames could not spread quickly between bushes.

Many valuable lessons came from that day, including my early retirement from the IED business. One lesson stands out: when we employ things in a context for which they were not originally intended, there can be devastating consequences. Fire, properly used, is an amazing thing. It provides warmth, enables us to cook food, propels powerful machinery, and provides beauty and ambiance. But when fire is neglected or misused, it can destroy homes, lay waste to entire cities, or be harnessed into a weapon of mass destruction.

Sex is similar to fire in that way. It is a wonderful gift from our heavenly Father; it was created by God for our good and his glory. It can bind husband and wife in ways that are mysterious and more intimate than any other human relationship, and it is the avenue by which human life is created. However, when it is taken out of its proper context, it devastates individual lives and families. Misused, sexuality can destroy lives, ruin relationships, and be weaponized in ways that lead to the corruption and demise of whole civilizations.

However, right now your concern is not saving the world; it is redeeming your marriage. Part of that redeeming process is coming to grips with and dealing with the losses, hurts, and pain caused by your pornography use. One significant, yet often overlooked, element to this process is known as lament.

Why put a chapter on lament in a book about redeeming a marriage hurt by pornography? Lament is an important part of the redemption/healing process when pornography has devastated lives. In this chapter, I hope to convince you of the value of grieving losses in general. More specifically, I want you to make sure that three kinds of grief are taking place in your home. First, let your wife grieve the losses and pain she has experienced because of your sin. Second, learn to grieve with her; show her the compassion of Christ during her suffering. Third, learn to grieve your own losses, especially the loss of innocence, which we will explore further later in this chapter.

Letting Her Lament

Has anyone ever betrayed your confidence? Maybe you had a friend in school that exposed your crush on a girl even though he swore that he would never tell. Perhaps you had a business partner who stole your ideas or work and used it to get a promotion that you deserved. Maybe you told a friend about a particular sin struggle, hoping that they would help you, but instead they spread the news through your friend group via the salacious gossip train. How hurt were you? How unloved did you feel? How betrayed did you feel? What did it do to your friendship? Do you still trust that person? Do you even want to see him anymore? Now amplify those feelings ten trillion times, and you can begin to relate to the pain that you have inflicted on your wife. Let her grieve that pain. It is important that you not only allow, but encourage, your wife to lament your sin and the impact it has had on her life.

As your wife grieves, you will need to give her space and time to do so. This may look like you silently supporting her in her grief. Pray to God silently in your heart on her behalf, and ask him to draw her near in his loving and protective arms. She will likely want and need to talk to someone else about the pain that she is feeling. Encourage her to do so. She is hurting because you have hurt her. Don't try to deny or downplay the pain. Encourage her to express it to a friend who can help bear her burden and point her to Christ. As she does this, she is not gossiping, but grieving. Encourage her to take her concerns and hurts to God, who cares for her far better than you or any other friend could.

As her heart softens, she may share with you how your sin has affected her. Don't get defensive; listen and learn from her. She may need an invitation to do this. Ask her, How has my sin affected you? What thoughts and feelings are you wrestling with? How has my sin brought temptation to you? She may not want to share with you at all. If that is the case, don't push. Let her know you are willing to listen when she is willing to talk. Tell her that you want to know so that you will grow in love and compassion as you seek to put off your self-focused sin. If she gets upset and lashes out at you, don't get defensive. Don't fight back. Recognize that hurting people often hurt people. She is hurting because of your sin, so it is no surprise that you are the target of her attacks. Pray for her. Cast your cares and her cares on the Lord because he cares for both of you (1 Peter 5:7). It may be best to have this kind of conversation with a spiritual mentor or biblical counselor present, but that is not always necessary. Ask God for wisdom and patience as she laments and heals. We will discuss forgiveness and reconciliation later. There may be things that your wife says or does in her pain that need to be dealt with, but in the lament process, don't focus on her sin; let her grieve yours. This is a great way to demonstrate that you love her and that you are genuinely grieved by your sin.

Lament with Her

"Weep with those who weep" (Romans 12:15). This short phrase is such a powerful one for the care of souls. Christ is the most compassionate person who ever walked the earth. Now that he has ascended back to his heavenly throne room, he has given us the wonderful responsibility and opportunity to be the physical manifestation of his compassionate love. As your wife shares how your sin has impacted her, let it sink into your heart. Try to put yourself in her shoes and feel her pain. Ask God to give you a soft heart so that you can feel what she feels. Compassion literally means to suffer together. Suffer with your wife in her suffering.

This will look differently for every couple, so don't try to use my suggestions as a strict template; instead, allow them to inspire and evoke your grieving process together. Always be sensitive to your wife's preferences at this time. Don't assume anything; instead ask. Ask questions such as the following: Do you want to share with me what you are thinking? Is it helpful for me to hold your hand? Would you rather write your words than speak them? Give preference to her desires (Philippians 2:3–4). When she shares her hurts, sit and listen. If she is crying, cry with her (don't try to force fake tears, but do allow her pain to impact you deeply, which, even if it doesn't result in actual tears, will create the true compassion at the heart of the command in Romans 12:15). If she is open to physical touch, embrace her and let her cry on your shoulder, or simply hold her hand while she weeps.

Lamenting Your Sin

Your wife should not be the only one grieving in this season. You also need to learn to grieve over your sin. Perhaps you already do. Hopefully the previous chapter helped you recognize the seriousness of the sins that you have committed against God and others (especially your wife). Perhaps that chapter simply reinforced truths you already know and feel. Or maybe you are just coming to grips with the depth of your sin. Either way, this is an opportunity for you to spend some additional time in lament to God.

James 4:8–10 shows us how part of drawing near to God is by turning away from sin. This involves mourning and weeping over our sin. The worldly sorrow drives people away from God in shame. Godly sorrow brings us to him. Go to him with the sorrow and grief you feel over your sin against him and the impact it has had on him (Isaiah 63:10; Ephesians 4:30) and those around you. Express in words what you are experiencing in your soul. What are you thinking, feeling, concerned about, afraid of, hoping for? Tell him. If you aren't broken and grieving over your sin, ask that he give you eyes to see your sin as he does. If you have never wept over your sin, ask him to soften your heart so that you are grieved by your sin as he is grieved over it. If you have never expressed compassion or empathy toward those your sin has hurt, ask that he give you a tender heart to feel their pain.

When you reflect back on the first time you were exposed to pornography, what do you think? What do you feel? Depending on where you are in this journey, you may actually think fondly of the time when you were introduced to something that brought you pleasure you had never known existed before. Most men that I've had the privilege of counseling through their struggle with pornography still remember the first time they were exposed to it. Sometimes it was through an intentional search for illicit images, but for most, it was a passive exposure. Maybe it was a forgotten scene in a movie that he watched with his parents, a stack of magazines he discovered while rifling through his brother's or father's closet, a website he stumbled upon while browsing the internet, or images a friend showed on his phone. For far too many, initiation into the world of sexuality did not come through images but through the sinful acts of sexual abuse by another (if this is your story please reach out to someone to talk to if you haven't already). However it happened, your first exposure to pornography or another sexual sin changed your life forever, and that change included loss and pain. Most of us look back and wish we had never sinned by using pornography. You see the chaos and hurt in you and around you that has been wreaked by your struggle with pornography, and you wish you could take it all back. But do you ever think of your initial exposure to pornography as a loss?

Lamenting Your Losses

In our culture we have a phrase, "the loss of innocence." It can be applied to a variety of situations: when our first pet dies, when we first experience the death of a loved one, and certainly whenever a person is first introduced to the world of pornography. When it comes to pornography, the loss of innocence is complicated. We lose innocence in the sense that our childish ignorance of sexuality is taken away, but we also lose innocence by (often) becoming complicit partakers in pornography after our initial exposure. The exposure awakens in us good, God-given desires, but they are awakened in a twisted way; they are awakened outside of the appropriate time and relationship for which they were intended.

God created sex. It is a good thing, a blessed gift from our heavenly Father that was meant to be enjoyed in the relationship of marriage. But taken out of that context, it is like a spark that flies out of a fireplace and sets a whole house ablaze. After that first exposure to pornography happened, your life was set on fire. It may have seemed like a tiny flame that was within your control, but you now realize that you played with fire and everyone around you has been burned. Your loss of innocence has led to many other losses, and those losses need to be grieved.[1]

In my counseling, I've found that many people have ungrieved losses that significantly inhibit their healing or growth. Although grieving is a key aspect of human existence, many do not know how to do it well. Lament is perhaps the most significant step or aspect of the grieving process. Lament is the action of bringing our griefs and sorrows to God. It is a dominant theme in the Psalms, and it is one that should permeate the lives of Christians. The key aspect of lament that sets it apart from mere complaint or self-pity is the direction of the heart. The lamenting person doesn't simply declare his complaints; he doesn't just wallow in his sadness and grief; and he doesn't weaponize his feelings against the one who inflicted the harm. The person who laments takes all their experiences to God and seeks to honor him through it all.

Lament is part of the process of grieving our losses, and laments contain complaints.[2] If that makes you uncomfortable, you are not alone. In my Christian upbringing, I was taught that the Bible says it's God's will for Christians to give thanks in all circumstances (1 Thessalonians 5:18) and to "Do all things without grumbling or disputing" (Philippians 2:14). At the same time, over one-third of the 150 Psalms are songs of lament. Since Scripture doesn't contradict itself, how are we to reconcile these responses to suffering that seem to contradict one another?

Here's the answer: There is a faithful type of prayer that voices the tension between pain and God's goodness.[3] It's called lament. Lament allows God's people to share their grievances and gratitude at the same time. As you practice lament, I hope you remember that you belong to a loving God who doesn't expect you to gloss over suffering. He invites you to communicate with him about your difficulties. Scripture is replete with examples of other Christians who have done the same (we even have an entire book in our Bibles called Lamentations). God welcomes us to grieve in his presence and honestly express the pain we face as a result of living in a fallen world.[4]

In his excellent book on grief, *God's Healing for Life's Losses*, Bob Kellemen demonstrates how the widely accepted five-stage model of grieving popularized by Elizabeth Kubler-Ross is an empty shell of the robust process of grieving that God provides for his children.[5] While the standard five stages leave us with mere acceptance of the circumstances, the grief process that God gives is designed to draw us closer to him. I highly recommend you read *God's Healing for Life's Losses* after you finish this book, especially if there is significant loss in your life.

I recommend that you talk to your counselor about this grief process and how it applies to you. You have losses in your life. Some were caused by your own sin, others were caused by someone else's sin, and some came in the natural course of living in a fallen world. All losses are worthy of grieving. Don't believe that because your loss is not as bad as someone else's or because it came as a result of your own sin that it doesn't matter to God. God doesn't sit up in heaven and say, "Only come to me with the problems you have that were inflicted upon you. The rest of the stuff, the problems you caused, go deal with them on your own." Nor does he say, "You got yourself into this mess, you get yourself out." Instead, he says, "bring all your cares to me because I care about you" (paraphrase of 1 Peter 5:7).

You can start this journey of grief by being real with yourself about the pain you have experienced. You may want to start by focusing on the pain you've gone through related to your sexual life: the pain of losing your sexual innocence, the pain of damaged relationships, the pain of having a good gift from God be twisted and misused, the pain of guilt and shame. Lift those losses to the Lord. Go to him and share your hurts. Ask your questions, and weep in his presence. He cares for you.

The way we approach God in prayer and lament is not going to be perfect. To foist such a demand on weary and heavy-laden souls is unloving and reminiscent of the Pharisees of Jesus's day. God invites his children to draw near, and he inclines himself toward them out of a deep, unconditional love for them, not on the basis of the quality of their approach. Don't try to clean yourself up before you go into his presence—just go. Don't think you have to approach him with some theologically informed, holy language; speak what is on your heart the way you normally speak. He hears all his children, no matter the child's language or maturity.

Questions for Action, Discussion, and Reflection

1. What has your grieving process been like in the past?

2. What significant losses have you experienced in your life? Make a list of these losses, and share the list with your biblical counselor or mentor. Ask them to help you begin to grieve those losses in a biblical way.

3. The biggest question that distinguishes lament from mere complaining is direction. Are you going to God with your concerns or grumbling to yourself and others? Are you being drawn closer to him in lament? Or is your complaint driving a wedge deeper and deeper between you and God?

Further Reading on Grief and Lament

Kellemen, Robert W. *God's Healing for Life's Losses: How to Find Hope When You're Hurting*. Winona Lake, IN: BMH Books, 2010.

Vroegop, Mark. *Dark Clouds, Deep Mercy: Discovering the Grace of Lament*. Wheaton, IL: Crossway, 2019.

3

Repentance

I LOST THIRTY pounds over my six-week stay at Lackland Air Force Base during basic military training. It wasn't that they didn't feed us (usually). It was the increased physical exertion through P.T. (physical training), marching, obstacle courses, etc. No matter how much I ate, I was constantly hungry. I could sit down, eat a full meal, then go stand in formation, and immediately my stomach would growl with hunger. Many parents comment that when their son returns from basic military training, he is not the same person as when he left, and they don't mean only physically. Basic training (aka boot camp) changes people. While my transformation did include a physical one, the changes wrought through the crucible of basic training go much deeper. It is a challenging, often grueling season physically, mentally, and spiritually. The outward transformation is the visible evidence of a deeper, inner change.

In a sense, my experience at basic training resembles repentance. It is an internal change that manifests in outward change. This chapter will focus on the inward change that we call repentance, and the next chapter will discuss some of the outward changes that we call the fruit of repentance.

Repentance is a word that, unfortunately, comes up far too little in our daily lives. If you grew up going to church, or if you have been around Christians long enough, you have probably heard the word. And you have probably heard some variation of this basic definition: Repentance means to turn around, to do a 180-degree turn away from sin. While this is certainly a good start to understanding the concept, it is incomplete. As you will see through this chapter, repentance is much more than a simple about-face from sin. It involves a complete transformation of our entire being, which includes our thoughts, beliefs, desires, affections, choices, etc. It is a necessary component of every significant relationship that we have and desire to keep. Repentance is foundational to Christian faith. Without repentance, there is no relationship with God, thus there is no salvation and no eternal life. Understanding and living this term is the distinction between eternal life or death.

The irony of the scarcity of this term in modern churches is that it was central to the message of Jesus during his earthly ministry. Jesus's predecessor and herald sent to prepare the way for his earthly ministry was John the Baptist. When John roamed the Judean wilderness announcing the coming Messiah, his message was, "Repent, for the kingdom of heaven is at hand" (Matthew 3:2). Jesus's very first words recorded in the gospel of Mark are "The time is fulfilled, and the kingdom of God is at hand; repent and believe in the gospel" (Mark 1:15). Similarly, when Matthew recounts the life of Jesus, he describes the launch of Jesus's public ministry in this way: "From that time Jesus began to preach, saying, 'Repent, for the kingdom of heaven is at hand'" (Matthew 4:17).

Not only was repentance central to Jesus's earthly ministry, it was also central to the subsequent ministry of his disciples. His initial followers—the disciples who went on to establish the church—continued to call people to repentance as a central piece of the message that they had inherited from the Lord. In the book of Acts, which recounts the founding of the early church, repentance is central. On the day of Pentecost, in response to Peter's first recorded sermon, the people ask "Brothers, what shall we do?" To this question Peter responds, "Repent and be baptized every one of you in the name of Jesus Christ for the forgiveness of your sins, and you will receive the gift of the Holy Spirit" (Acts 2:37–38).

Repentance is essential to the gospel. Perhaps you are reading this and you aren't even sure what the gospel is, or maybe you have heard that term and understand the concept, but you haven't yet believed the message of the gospel. I have good news for you—today could be the beginning of a whole new life for you, if you will believe. Even if you are a believer in Jesus or are well acquainted with the gospel, I encourage you not to skip this section. Keep reading. There may be some insight offered you haven't considered before, and even if there is not, renewing your mind daily with the gospel is always a good idea.

The simple definition of the word *gospel* is good news. As a matter of fact, it is the best news ever! In order for you to understand why, we have to go back in time, to the very beginning of time.

Repentance for Salvation

The Bible teaches us that God created the universe in six days simply by the awesome power of his will. He spoke everything into existence out of nothing. On the last day of his creative work, he made the first man, Adam (Genesis 1). Then God made the first woman, Eve, to be his companion and wife (Genesis 2). Initially, this couple was perfect; they had done nothing to violate God's perfect will. But that didn't last long. Satan came into the beautiful garden that God had created for Adam and Eve and tempted Eve to disobey God. She gave into the temptation, violating God's law, and then she invited her husband, who was with her, to do the same (Genesis 3). Adam followed suit and ate the forbidden fruit, violating God's perfect law. Failing to live up to God's perfect standard is called sin. Prior to sin, they lived in perfect harmony with one another and with God. After sin, they were separated from God. Through Adam and Eve's sin, the entire human race was cut off from close fellowship and union with God. God made a promise that one day he would provide a bridge to rectify the gulf that separated humanity from himself (Genesis 3:15). The problem was that separation caused by sin could only be overcome by the willing blood sacrifice of the life of a *perfect* human being (Hebrews 9:22). In order to accomplish this, God had to become man because all of us born in the line of Adam and Eve are sinners by nature.

Millennia after God first promised to send a Redeemer who could bridge the chasm that divided man from God, Jesus was born to a poor carpenter's family from an obscure village in the tiny nation of Israel. Jesus was miraculously conceived in his virgin mother Mary's womb, the one-of-a-kind Son of God (John 3:16), who was perfect and untainted by sin. Jesus grew up much as all of us did, in a family with brothers and sisters, an imperfect set of parents, spending his time attending school and learning a trade. He experienced all the temptations and trials of this life, but he never once sinned (Matthew 4:1–11; Hebrews 4:15). When he was about thirty years of age, he began publicly preaching the message that we read above: "Repent, for the kingdom of heaven is at hand." Many were drawn to listen to his message. Some believed it, others rejected it, and some were so angered by it that they determined to kill him—and they eventually succeeded. After around three years of public ministry, Jesus was arrested on trumped-up charges, abandoned by all his friends, rushed through an illegal trial, tortured, and then executed as a capital criminal by one of the cruelest forms of execution ever devised—crucifixion.

However, the sinless, divine Jesus could not be held by death. He rose from the grave three days after his burial, thereby conquering sin and death. Weeks later, he ascended into heaven to sit at the right hand of the throne of God.

Because of his momentous work he freely offers eternal life and so much more to all those who will simply turn from their sin and put their faith in him. When we do that, we are changed forever, brought into the family of God as heirs with Jesus (Romans 8:17). He becomes our advocate, standing in for us when we sin, praying for us, comforting us with his spirit, leading and guiding us, transforming us to be more and more like him (Romans 8:28–30; 1 John 2:1). He chooses us and then sends us out as ambassadors for his kingdom (John 15:16–19; 2 Corinthians 5:20). He becomes our greatest ally in the fight against sin. All this, and more, happens the moment we repent and believe.

Elements of Repentance

Metanoia is the Greek word in the New Testament translated as repentance. A simple definition of the word is to "turn around, change one's mind, repent."[1] While the word may have a simple definition, the biblical concept of repentance cannot be contained in such a small phrase. One theologian identifies three elements of the biblical concept of repentance: the intellectual, the emotional, and the volitional.[2]

The Intellectual Element of Repentance

The intellectual element of repentance involves a change in our thinking and understanding about sin and our relationship to it. We learn the truth about sin from God's Word and then put off false ideas we've learned or believed in the past. This could come through simple biblical instruction that awakens someone to the reality that their desires or actions are sinful. My uncle was once leading a junior high boys' Bible study when a new young man raised a bizarre request during prayer time. He wanted to pray and ask God to help him "score" with his girlfriend that weekend. As an unbeliever, or perhaps a new Christian, the boy had no idea that sex outside of marriage was wrong. For him, the intellectual element of repentance involved learning and adopting the biblical standard for sexuality.

In some cases, the intellectual element of repentance begins with the acknowledgment that there is right and wrong. Moral relativism has permeated our culture, resulting in many people rejecting the idea that there are absolute moral guidelines. Instead, they believe that everyone should be able to do whatever they want, whenever they want, with whomever they want. Meanwhile, those who believe there are moral rights and wrongs may still have faulty thinking when it comes to sin. They may see sins simply as mistakes or perhaps blame the wrong things they do on their upbringing or genetics: "I learned this from my dad," or "I can't help it; I was born this way." Excuses for sin or attempts to minimize/alter their severity are endless.

When God grants us true repentance, all that goes away. We gain a true knowledge of sin and understand that we are guilty of violating his perfect law, that we deserve condemnation and punishment for our sin, and that we are helpless to do anything about it on our own (Romans 1:32; 3:20). As it relates to you and your use of pornography, true repentance means that you can't try to excuse it because of some past experience, blame it on your parents, or attribute it to your genes. You can't believe that pornography is no big deal, or that it is art, or that you are just admiring God's creation. You can't fall into the pattern of our first parents by blaming it on your wife, even if she encouraged you to use pornography (Genesis 3:12). You can't justify it by saying "It's okay to look as long as you don't touch." You must acknowledge and believe that it is sinful, a violation of God's law, because it is mental adultery.

The intellectual element of repentance is vital. We must align our thinking to God's way of thinking about reality and about our sin. And yet, while the intellectual element is vital, it is not sufficient on its own. Without the emotional and volitional elements, knowledge of sin alone often turns into fear of being caught or fear of punishment, but it does not produce a genuine hatred of the sin.

The Emotional Element of Repentance

The emotional element of repentance involves feeling sorrow over the sins we have committed against our loving and holy God, as well as overwhelming joy at the prospect of his forgiving love (Psalm 51). When David wrote this psalm of genuine repentance and its companion, Psalm 32, he used incredibly emotive language. In his writing, he describes the tremendous weight of guilt that rested on him before he turned from his sin: "For when I kept silent, my bones wasted away through my groaning all day long. For day and night your hand was heavy upon me; my strength was dried up as by the heat of summer" (Psalm 32:3–4). That same Psalm ends with joyous celebration and relief because of God's forgiveness: "Many are the sorrows of the wicked, but steadfast love surrounds the one who trusts in the LORD. Be glad in the LORD, and rejoice, O righteous, and shout for joy, all you upright in heart!" (Psalm 32:10–11). When the emotional element of repentance is combined with the intellectual and volitional elements of repentance, it becomes what 2 Corinthians 7 describes as "godly grief," and it leads to life. Without the other elements, it often manifests as "worldly grief" and leads to death (2 Corinthians 7:10). "Worldly grief" may have all the external displays of sorrow, tears, guilt, and promises to change, but it doesn't result in true change.

The Volitional Element of Repentance

The volitional element of repentance involves a change in our will. We turn our purpose, desires, longings, and choices away from sin and to the cleansing power of Christ's blood, seeking to live a life worthy of his calling (Ephesians 4:1). This element is empowered and driven by the other two. Our emotions are powerful motivators fueled by our beliefs. When the two work together, they can steer our desires, choices, and actions. If any element of repentance is missing, it is not genuine repentance and will not result in a changed life.

Underlying and Accompanying Sins

When it comes to pornography use, it is easy to assume that we need to change our thoughts, emotions, and choices away from the sin of lust. While this is certainly part of the journey, it is important to recognize that other underlying sins may be driving you to pursue pornography and sins that are common companions of pornography.

We all have the general tendency to seek pleasure and avoid pain. In the Psalms, God is described more than 100 times as a refuge, a place of comfort and safety from the trials of life. When difficult times come, we are to turn to him to find peace and comfort for our souls. However, we are foolish, sinful people who like to do things on our own, and we like quick fixes. So instead of turning to the Rock of Ages as our stronghold and refuge, as the true source of lasting peace for our souls, we run to things that will give us a quick, temporary rush of pleasure. These false refuges often distract us from our pain or mask the turmoil inside—at least for a while. For some, it is a substance, such as alcohol or drugs, that give a buzz, a high, or completely blanks out the mind for a while. For others, it could be eating certain foods. Have you ever considered that we have a whole category of food we call "comfort food"? Chocolate, sugar, and high fat foods all taste delicious and get those pleasure sensations pumping. Also, of course, there is sex. Few things give such an intense rush of pleasure as an orgasm. In the right context, most of these things are delights that we are intended to enjoy. They are gifts from our Creator who likes to give good gifts to his children (Matthew 7:11; Luke 11:13). He created us to experience pleasure and delight in his creation—but only in ways that draw us to him in worship. When we use those good gifts to alleviate or mask our pain, we are using them to do something that only God can do. We have supplanted the creator with his creation. When we run to these things perpetually, we develop what is commonly called an addiction. Rather than enjoying these good gifts and thanking God for them in joyful worship, we become enslaved to them (Romans 6:16–23, 7:14–25). For you, pornography has most likely become a false refuge. You may have other "refuges" as well, so be on the alert.

What is it that causes you distress in life? What brings about the pain that drives you to find peace or pleasure? Answering these questions can help delve into some of the underlying sins that lead you to pornography use (or the pursuit of other false refuges). Perhaps you run to pornography when you feel rejected. Maybe this comes when your wife turns down your sexual advances, or maybe rejection hits you when you see a friend's social media post about a party that you weren't invited to. Your prideful heart can turn a good desire for love and acceptance into a demand for approval, acceptance, and praise. When you don't get those things, or you don't get them in the way you want them, you can be tempted to find acceptance elsewhere. The allure of porn offers you not only the rush of pleasure from sexual arousal and orgasm, but it also gives you a false sense of acceptance from a whole host of women who are always available. They never say no, they never turn you down, and they never reject you. You ultimately need to address your feelings of rejection not with a harem of endlessly aroused women, but with a God who is inclined to you—a God who understands your hurts and never turns away from you; a God who accepts you and invites you to come to him in your times of trouble (Hebrews 4:16).

Another common allure to pornography is the sense of power it gives. Perhaps you feel powerless in your work or in your family life. You get passed over for promotions, your ideas get rejected, and no one seems to listen to you. Your wife may have a big personality and strong opinions, and you find yourself giving in to her desires and demands all the time. Or maybe you feel disrespected and torn down by her constant criticism. You want a place where you can be in charge. You want people who will take you seriously and do what you say. Pornography is where you find your power.

Likewise, a desire for control can tempt some to pornography. If your life seems totally chaotic and out of control, you might find pleasure in the sense of control that pornography promises. When markets fluctuate, disease dominates, and relationships are unstable, porn may seem like something that is a constant. You know where to go, how to get there, what to expect, and what you will get in the end. However, as you probably already know, it doesn't ultimately come through on that promise, you aren't in control when you become pornography's slave. The only one who is in control, the only one you can put full trust and confidence in, is our Lord and Savior who is the same yesterday, today, and forever (Hebrews 13:8).

In addition to sinful desires that motivate your pornography use, there are many other sins that accompany it. Giving into desires that you know are sinful demonstrates a lack of self-control. While I'm not trying to promote a "pull yourself up by your bootstraps," "you can do it!" Christianity, self-control is part of the fruit of the Spirit (Galatians 5:22-23). Ironically, lack of self-control is a demonstration that you are trying to go it alone instead of walking by the Spirit.

Deception is another sin that accompanies pornography use. Manifestations of deception while using pornography include outright lies denying that you are viewing it, partial-truth confessions of sin, and various methods used to cover your tracks or hide your use. Putting on the truth and being fully known are important elements of the transformation you are seeking.

Digging into underlying and accompanying sins that may be intermingled with your porn use will help you on a deeper level to overcome your desire for pornography. A biblical counselor or spiritual mentor can help you explore these sins. The reality is that if you don't address these deeper issues and learn to run to God as your constant source of refuge and peace, you may manage to put off pornography use, but you will just replace it with another false refuge. Only in a continual, day by day, deepening relationship with Jesus will you find lasting peace.

Walking in Repentance

Before you leave this chapter thinking that changing is all about you pulling yourself up by your own bootstraps, I must remind you that saving faith and repentance are gifts from God. You are probably exhausted over this struggle. You have probably tried before to put off this sin. You may feel tired, lost, overwhelmed, and maybe even hopeless. I know that feeling too. I've been there, and I know it can tempt you to give up. I hope that these next few paragraphs will encourage you not to give up.

You are in a war. Wars are fought in skirmishes and battles. Sometimes you will win them, other times you will lose them. The response to either outcome is to keep fighting. When you win a skirmish with temptation, when you click away from that enticing advertisement instead of gazing at it or clicking on it, praise the Lord and keep pressing forward. When you lose the battle and lust after that image, don't throw in the towel and give up—instead, keep fighting, keep pressing forward. If you are fighting with Christ and his Spirit on your side, then the ultimate victory is secured.

Some people will achieve total victory over pornography in this lifetime. They are like those who can go cold turkey off a substance and never look back. But that is not the case for most of us. The battle against pornography, against any sin, is a lifelong journey of renewing repentance. And even those who never again sin by looking at pornography will be tempted and sin in other ways. There is the once-for-all shift in you that we discussed above, the repentance that leads to salvation, but there is also the regular practice of identifying, acknowledging, and turning away from ongoing sin in our lives.

Common Misconceptions About Repentance

Common misconceptions about repentance and growth often compound our battle with pornography. We often hold and promote the idea that we can achieve perfection (at least over particular sins) at some point in this life. Sometimes we perpetuate this idea in the way we talk about and address sin from the pulpit or in the counseling room when we talk about our struggle with a particular sin only in the past tense. Most of the books I read on pornography were written by men who declared that they had struggled with it at some point in the past. It seemed really transparent and vulnerable to share that they had struggled with this dark sin, but none shared from the perspective of a current/ongoing struggle with the sin. For many men, this can be very discouraging. It is encouraging to hear that pornography use can be overcome. However, it is discouraging for men who have struggled—and struggled for years while thinking that the goal is a life free of temptation or without the need for persistent vigilance in this area. When pastors, church leaders, authors, and biblical counselors who have wrestled with pornography in the past act as though there is no ongoing battle, they don't serve the majority of men I have encountered; they give them false hope or set a false standard.

The prior misconception is related to the misconception that victory over pornography means that we would someday achieve a level of spirituality where we are no longer enticed by lustful images. It is the idea that victory means a lack of temptation. However, that is not what God promises, or expects. Because Jesus experienced temptation (Matthew 4; Hebrews 4:15) we know that temptation is not failure. Temptation is not sin. Victory over temptation is not the absence of temptation but facing temptation and not giving into it. Victory is resisting or running from temptation so that it doesn't lead to sin (Ephesians 6:11; 2 Timothy 2:22; James 1:14–15). Victory over porn doesn't mean you will never be tempted to lust.

Walking in victory over pornography is about your ongoing, daily walk with Jesus. It is the daily renewal of your commitment to die to yourself, turn from sin, say no to temptation, and say yes to him (Luke 9:23). It involves deepening your relationship with Jesus and your other allies in this journey of life. Ultimate victory is already secured by Christ. Victory in our daily, weekly, and monthly battles with porn and other sins depends on Christ as well. When we are walking with him by the Spirit, we will not walk according to our fleshly desires (Galatians 5:16–26).

Hebrews 12:2 calls Jesus the founder and perfecter of our faith. He is the one who began it, and he is the one who will bring it to completion. If you have repented of your sin before God and put your faith in Jesus, it is because he put the inclination and ability within you to turn from sin and walk in righteousness. He promises to keep you in the race, moving forward. "I am sure of this, that he who began a good work in you will bring it to completion at the day of Jesus Christ" (Philippians 1:6). The apostle Paul was inspired by God to write those words and then moments later to write, "work out your own salvation with fear and trembling, for it is God who works in you, both to will and to work for his good pleasure" (Philippians 2:12–13). There is a mysterious cooperation at work in our repentance. We are called to work hard at living for God, all the while acknowledging that he is the one who gives us the ability and motivation to do so. You may at some point in this life be free from any temptation to indulge in pornography; I pray that is someday true for you and for me. But one thing I know for sure—that battle will end when I see Jesus face to face. At that moment, I will be fully like him. The slow, steady process of sanctification that began when I repented and put my faith in Jesus will come to completion, and I will be fully transformed into his image (1 John 3:2). Keep running the race, keep fixing your eyes on Jesus, and keep giving him all the praise.

Questions for Action, Discussion, and Reflection

1. What do you think about your sin? Do you think you are a sinner? What do you believe that means about you, your relationship with God, and the eternal state of your soul?

2. If you are convinced that you need to repent and turn to Christ for the first time, call your counselor or another Christian friend right now and share this news with him.

3. How do you feel about your sin? Do you feel sorrow over your sin? Does it make you angry when you sin? Are you indifferent about your sin?

4. What are your desires and wishes regarding pornography? Do you wish to continue in your sin or forsake it and turn toward Christ?

5. What underlying and accompanying sins do you wrestle with related to your pornography use?

6. If you are convinced that you need to put off a particular sin or sins, confess that to God in prayer. Ask him to give you the strength and courage to turn away from your sin and toward Christ.

Further Reading on Repentance

Lane, Timothy S., and Paul David Tripp. *How People Change.* 2nd ed. Greensboro, NC: New Growth Press, 2008.

Miller, C. John. *Repentance: A Daring Call to Real Surrender.* Fort Washington, PA: CLC Publications, 2019.

4

The Fruits of Repentance

DURING THE MAJORITY of the time a recruit spends in basic training for the military they are called "Trainee." You must refer to yourself as "Trainee (insert your last name)." Any time you wish to speak to your drill instructor (DI) you must say, "Sir, Trainee Solomon, reports," or if the DI initiated the conversation, you must respond, "Trainee Solomon reports, as ordered." Your drill instructors beat this response into your head over and over and over again. Even though you enlisted to become a soldier, sailor, airman, or marine, you cannot adopt that title until you have earned it. At a certain stage of basic training, near the end, trainees have earned the right to be called by the distinguishing title of their branch of service. But in order to reach that phase of training, one must demonstrate a pattern of living consistent with that title. You cannot call yourself *airman* until you have shown by your life that you know what it means to be one.

Repentance is similar. You cannot simply claim to be repentant; your life must demonstrate genuine repentance by bearing fruit consistent with a repentant heart (Matthew 3:8; Luke 3:8). Whether you just came to saving faith or have been a follower of Christ for some time, your life should bear the fruit of repentance. Like repentance, bearing the fruit of repentance is something that happens continually throughout life. While quite a variety of specific fruits are born in each person's life, several common themes should be present in every manifestation of genuine repentance: confession, forsaking of sin, restitution/ reconciliation if necessary, and pursuit of righteousness. We will deal specifically with reconciliation later, because it requires us to understand the biblical principles surrounding forgiveness, which will be dealt with in the next chapter. In the remainder of this chapter, we will address confession and forsaking of sin.

While genuine repentance is an inward act, it is not one that can remain internal—it must influence the way we live our lives. As Berkhof wrote in *Systematic Theology*, "The Bible describes repentance as an internal act, but it is one that necessarily results in certain actions and an overall transformation of the way one lives."[1] A changed life springs forth from the inward changes in our beliefs, desires, and affections toward sin. When someone comes to saving faith, when they respond to Jesus's call to repent and believe, these changes happen internally, but these internal changes lead to an outward confession of our sinful state before God and man. Genuine repentance also leads to a life that forsakes old sinful habits and behaviors and pursues a life of righteousness and good works for God's glory (Ephesians 2:10).

Since you are reading this book because of a struggle with pornography, you certainly need to practice ongoing repentance in this area of your life. But pornography is not your only sin. It is not the only thing you struggle with and need to forsake. Those of us who struggle with porn face the temptation to believe the lie that porn is the only problem (or the most significant problem) in our lives. We can be tempted to base our assessment of life, our spiritual maturity, our standing with God, and our love for our spouse all on how well we are doing in this one area of life. That can lead to more problems—including legalism, self-righteousness, depression, and ignoring other sins that need attention.

Confessing Sin

The first fruit of repentance is confession—the outward acknowl-edgment of sin. 1 John 1:9 says, "If we confess our sins, he is faithful and just to forgive us our sins and to cleanse us from all unrighteousness." The Greek word translated as "confess" has the literal meaning "to say the same thing" or "to agree to something."[2] While the word has taken on many nuanced appli-cations, the central point of "agreement" remains. When we con-fess our sins to God, we are agreeing with him about what we have done. When we confess to another the sin that we have com-mitted against them, we are agreeing with that person about what has taken place. When we try to make excuses for our sin or call it something other than sin, we are not truly confessing. If you try to explain away your pornography as some kind of disease, a simple mistake, admiration of God's created beauty, or anything else other than sinful lust, you have not truly confessed your sin. When we truly repent, our hearts admit the true nature of our sin-fulness and our sin. That leads us to verbal confession—acknowl-edging that sin to God and to those we have sinned against. We come to an agreement with them about the true nature of our soul and the sin that we committed against them.

In a couple of key passages in the book of Matthew, Jesus teaches us how to handle sin between people. In Matthew 5:23–24 he instructs us on properly handling our sin against another person, and in Matthew 18:15–20 he tells us how to handle situ-ations where someone sins against us. Both situations involve at least one conversation. We will discuss these conversations fur-ther in the next chapter on forgiveness, but for now, I want you to see that repentance leads to conversations where sin is identified and owned as a violation of God's perfect standard.

When it comes to your struggle with pornography, you need to have at least one conversation where you fully disclose your entire struggle to your wife. If your sin has already been revealed to your wife, it came through either discovery or disclosure. She either found out about it on her own, or you opened up and shared your struggle with her. If, by chance, your wife has no idea about your current struggle, you should let her know sooner rather than later. I recommend you connect with a biblical counselor and request counseling for your pornography struggle. Let him know you have not told your wife and ask him to help you craft an initial confession to your wife and find a biblical counselor for her. The initial confession will be general and vague. You will need to let her know that you have been struggling with pornography and that you are seeking help and you want to make sure she is getting the care she needs as well.

Full disclosure is a sensitive matter and can cause further harm if handled inappropriately. The best context for the two of you to grow will be with a male biblical counselor for you and a female biblical counselor for your wife, who are part of your local church. If your pastor does not provide counseling and you don't have any biblical counselors in your local church, you can find some by visiting the counselor directories from various biblical counseling ministries. The Biblical Counseling Coalition's website lists counselors and also links to the directories of other biblical counseling ministries.

Wherever you find them, be sure you have a biblical counselor for each of you before a full disclosure meeting. Again, the most ideal situation is to receive care in the context of the local church, but if that is not an option don't worry; there are plenty of great biblical counselors and God is used to working in amazing ways in less-than-ideal situations.

Regardless of who you ask to help you with this conversation, a central goal to keep in mind is disclosing the depth and breadth of your sin without including all the details. Your wife needs to know enough to understand your situation and how to help, but she does not need to be burdened with details that will make forgiveness and reconciliation unnecessarily hard. For instance, she needs to know where, when, and how often you have accessed pornography, but she doesn't need to know details about the sizes and shapes of the bodies you lusted after. If your wife asks for these types of details, your biblical counselors can intervene. He can let her know you are not trying to be elusive, but that those details will hinder the process, not help it. If your wife raises questions about details and specifics outside of your full disclosure conversation, you can also tell her that you will ask your biblical counselor whether it would be helpful for her to know the information she is requesting. Affirm your commitment to be open and honest, but remind her that having those details is not serving any good purpose.

When it comes to a full disclosure conversation, it is often helpful to write a letter to your wife, fully explaining the extent of your sin and its impacts as well as you can. You will need to address specifics of your struggle with pornography (see the following list of questions), and you will also want to confess in your letter any other sins associated with your pornography use. This should include any deception, selfishness, ways you have not proactively loved your wife, the time/energy/resources wasted on sinful pursuits, leading your wife to use pornography if you have done so, pride, laziness, etc. Share how you see your sin impacting her and your family and describe how you desire to grow and change with God's help.

After you have written the letter, have your biblical counselor review the letter and offer suggestions. Edit the letter in accordance with the suggestions, and have the biblical counselor review the letter again. Keep editing it until the biblical counselor agrees that it is appropriate to share. Of course, don't write things you do not believe simply to comply with your counselor's suggestions; the letter needs to be genuine and honest. Once the letter is complete, come together with your wife and your biblical counselors to read the letter to her. The four of you should agree on a time for this in advance so she and her biblical counselor can begin to prepare her heart and she is not caught off guard.

Here are some questions that your wife should know the answers to (they are also included in the companion book, *Reclaim Your Marriage: Grace for Wives Who Have Been Hurt by Pornography*):

1. Where do you go to find pornographic media (i.e. specific websites, social media outlets, streaming services, magazines, mail catalogs, etc.)?
2. Has the sin of porn use been accompanied by other forms of sexual sin (e.g. strip clubs, masturbation, prostitutes, online sexual interactions with women or men)? If your sexual sin has crossed over into physical acts with another person, you need to immediately address that with your biblical counselor. There are specific considerations in that case that are outside the scope of this book.
3. Have you spent any money on sexual experiences? If so, when, how, and how much money?
4. What other sins has your porn use fostered (e.g. lying, abusing alcohol or drugs to numb the guilt, etc.)?
5. Are there other forms of excessive indulgence that often precede or follow your porn use (e.g. overspending, overeating, drunkenness, etc.)?
6. Have you ever viewed homosexual, child, or violent porn? If you have viewed pornography involving children or acts of violence, tell your biblical counselor right away. Cooperate fully with their counsel, and submit yourself to any legal scrutiny that may come. I know this will be difficult, but God will be most glorified, and you will be most helped, by full,

honest confession and submission to the authorities that God has placed over you.

7. What scenarios provide the greatest temptation toward sexual sin (e.g., at work on the night shift, alone at home for the weekend while your spouse travels, on overnight business trips, after a stressful day at work, etc.)?

8. When and where are you viewing porn?

9. How many times a day/week/month/year are you viewing porn?

10. How long do you view porn per session?

11. How often do you masturbate?

12. What specific lies have you told to hide your porn use?

13. Have you found or utilized any loopholes within the safeguards that are currently used to keep your electronic devices free of porn? If so, explain.

14. Does any sin come to mind that you have yet to confess?

When you come together for the meeting, let your biblical counselor take the lead, open in prayer, and then invite you to read your letter. The biblical counselor will often take some time at that point to let your wife ask questions. If she has questions, allow the biblical counselor time to intervene, in case the questions are unhelpful. Then answer her questions honestly. She may not have questions at this time; every wife will respond in her own way. Before the meeting ends, let her know you want to ask forgiveness, but you want to wait until she has had time to process and think about other impacts/implications of your sin. You can tell her that at some point in the future, when she has had time to process and the Lord has prepared her heart, you would like to ask her forgiveness. Your counselors may ask you to leave the room so that your wife can talk with them privately. Don't be alarmed by this, and don't fight it. Give her space and time to ask questions and receive answers and care. This is a very painful time for both of you, and it is a good opportunity for you to walk in repentance by demonstrating care for her concerns over your own.

The follow-up conversation where you ask forgiveness should also be conducted with your biblical counselors present. We will explore that conversation in more detail in the next chapter.

Forsaking Sin

The second fruit of repentance is forsaking your sin. Your inward U-turn away from sin must manifest in an outward U-turn as well. If your buddy came to you and said he had finally made the decision to change from couch potato to athlete, that would be great. But if weeks went by without him ever going to the gym or out for a run, you would know that no real change had occurred. If you tell yourself, God, and your wife that you finally realized it is wrong for you to view pornography, but then you keep watching it all the same, it will be hard for them to believe you have truly repented. Forsaking sin is the first part of the larger practice of sanctification. Sanctification involves both putting off sin and putting on a righteous alternative. The Bible offers lots of specific insight to help us fight particular sins, as well as general principles that can be applied to our battle with every sin.

A simple acronym to help you remember some key principles for fighting sin is AAA. AAA stands for admiration, accountability, and amputation. Now don't confuse a simple memory tool with a simplistic solution. AAA is easy to say and remember, but far more challenging to live out. Chapters 6 through 9 of this book will dive into each of these aspects of forsaking sin and show you how to flesh them out in your own life.

I have described repentance as a U-turn away from sin. Like the U-turns we make while driving down the road, the U-turn of repentance is not only turning way from something, but it is turning toward something. We turn away from sin and move in the opposite direction. We turn away from self-worship and turn toward true worship of God. We turn away from lying and turn toward telling the truth (Ephesians 4:25). We turn away from stealing and turn toward working hard so that we can share with those in need (Ephesians 4:28). We put off our old selves and put on a new way of living (Ephesians 4:20–24).

Forsaking sin means turning away from wickedness and turning toward righteousness. As you seek to put off pornography and all its associated sinful attitudes and actions, you must replace them with God-honoring attitudes and actions. Instead of selfish lust, you should put on selfless love. Rather than filling your mind with impure images, you should engage your thoughts with things that are true, honorable, just, pure, lovely, excellent, and worthy of praise (Philippians 4:8).

As you work with your counselor, consider all the underlying and accompanying sins associated with your pornography use. Discuss ways of putting them off as well as what righteous replacements you can put on in their place.

What about Relapse?

While genuine repentance does involve a turn away from sin in our attitudes and actions, recurrence of that sin in our lives does not necessarily mean that our repentance was inauthentic or otherwise faulty. There are some who hold to this strict view of repentance. Often, they are motivated by a false application of verses like 1 John 3:6 and 9 which say, "No one who abides in him keeps on sinning; no one who keeps on sinning has either seen him or known him. . . . No one born of God makes a practice of sinning, for God's seed abides in him, and he cannot keep on sinning because he has been born of God."

Taken at face value, these verses would not only call into question the genuine repentance of a man who relapses into porn use, but it would also call into question the salvation of anyone who sins post-conversion. I won't take time to fully develop all of the arguments against this interpretation, but one way we know John is not advocating for perfection is that a perfectionist interpretation would contradict much of the rest of his letter. Earlier in the letter John states, "My little children, I am writing these things to you so that you may not sin. But if anyone does sin, we have an advocate with the Father, Jesus Christ the righteous" (1 John 2:1). If John expected sinless perfection after someone came to saving faith, then we would not need Jesus as our advocate.

The misconception that perfect obedience is the only evidence of genuine repentance leaves people discouraged. Most people who struggle with enslaving sins, or what we often describe as addictions (Romans 6; Hebrews 12:1), will continue to struggle with them. Sometimes people do experience a radical deliverance from their sinful habits and never return to them again (praise the Lord for those times). But that is not the typical journey for most Christians. For many who struggle with pornography, giving into the temptation to look at porn is extremely discouraging, especially after a long period of faithfulness in this area. It can raise doubts about the genuineness of one's repentance and even salvation (both in the mind of the struggler and in the minds of those they hurt with their sin). It can also feel like those instances of returning to our sin take us back to ground zero and we are starting all over again. The image of repentance in the Bible is not someone who turns away from sin and never looks back, but someone who changes their orientation to sin and then repeatedly fights to keep moving away from it. If perfect obedience post-conversion is the measurement of genuine faith, then no one would be saved. God does not save us by grace alone, through faith alone, in Christ alone, and then demand that we walk in perfect obedience to keep our salvation (Galatians 3:3).

The sad truth is that you are likely to return to pornography. I don't want to discourage you by raising this possibility or offer you an excuse for your sin, but I also want to be honest about the struggle. Honesty and transparency will encourage us and empower us in this fight. If we set our hope and expectation on perfect behavior moving forward, we are going to be less likely to confess our temptations and failures which, in turn, will make us more vulnerable to further enslavement. If we instead fix our eyes on Jesus, the one who starts our story and the one who finishes it, we will be motivated to keep running the race, both when it is smooth sailing and when we are barely stumbling along (Hebrews 12:1–2).

Pursuing Sanctification: the Process of Growth, Change, and Transformation

The line of sanctification is a jagged up and down climb, not either immediate transport to perfection, nor a smooth straight climb. But the downward slides don't take us all the way to the bottom of the mountain.

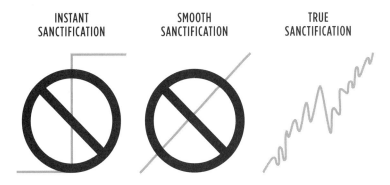

INSTANT SANCTIFICATION SMOOTH SANCTIFICATION TRUE SANCTIFICATION

Sanctification is a big word we use to describe the process of being made more and more like Jesus. When God first created Adam and Eve, they were made "in his own image" (Genesis 1:27). The word used for "image" in that passage was often used in the ancient Near East to describe a statue of a ruler that would be put in the center of a city that was under his control. In one way,

God was setting human beings on the earth as a way of saying, "I rule here." But when Adam and Eve sinned, the image of God was marred. Imagine the statue being toppled from its pedestal and breaking into millions of pieces. The essence of the image is still there, but it is unrecognizable as the image of the ruler. Before we come to saving faith, we are like that broken statue. When we come to saving faith, it is as if Jesus gathers all those pieces and begins gluing them back together. Sanctification is the process of being glued back together so that we can more fully reflect God's image. The longer we are walking with God, the more we look like Jesus. The more he works in our lives, the more pieces of his image come back together.

Turning away from sin and pursuing righteousness is part of this sanctification process. It is totally dependent upon your deepening relationship with Jesus. When you are climbing the upward slope of the mountain of life and you start to slip backward, you must rely on your guide and your equipment. Jesus is there to grab hold of you, pull you up, and help you keep moving forward. Even in the moments where we feel relatively independent, as though we can handle things on our own, we need to realize that he is the one who paved the way, he is the one who holds the safety line, and he is the one who motivates us to move forward. Every moment of forward or upward progress is empowered by him, and every fall downhill is met with his helping hand to lift us up and guide us onward.

As you turn away from sin and turn toward righteousness, you will need to pursue reconciliation with those who have been impacted by your sin. The U-turn away from self-love and self-worship means turning toward love of others and worship of God. Reconciliation requires forgiveness, which is the topic of the next chapter.

Questions for Action, Discussion, and Reflection

1. Is there evidence of genuine repentance in your life? If so, what are the visible fruits that have grown from your repentance?

2. If you have experienced relapses into pornography, how have those times impacted your view of yourself and your understanding of your relationship with God? How has this chapter helped adjust your thinking on that matter?

3. If you need to confess your sin to someone or make a full disclosure to your spouse, write out what you are thinking and then share it with your biblical counselor. Ask them to help you express this confession well and then to help you walk in newness of life.

Further Reading

Powlison, David. *How Does Sanctification Work?* Wheaton: Crossway, 2017.

5

Forgiveness

CARRIE UNDERWOOD'S SONG "Before He Cheats" expresses the thoughts, feelings, and desires of many women who have been betrayed. Her lyrics express the common desire for revenge when we have been wronged. Someone has harmed me, and I want to hurt them back. Most of us can acknowledge a certain degree of empathy with these feelings. We recognize a serious offense has taken place, a wrong has been done, an injustice has occurred. We want justice; we want the wrong to be righted; we want to blot out the offense. However, we also recognize that vengeance is not justice, and responding to sin with further sin does not resolve a situation but makes it worse. Instead, forgiveness is God's solution to injustice and the path toward reconciliation and reunion after sin has separated a relationship.

You may wonder why I am writing a chapter on forgiveness when your wife is the one who will need the instruction on how to forgive. First, you need to know what you are asking for when you ask your wife to forgive you. Second, you need to support and encourage your wife in her work to forgive you, so you need to understand what forgiveness is. Third, while we are primarily addressing your sin in this book, you will undoubtedly be sinned against in this life, and I want you to know how to respond properly in those situations. Fourth, a lot of bad information exists about forgiveness, and I like to correct it as much as possible every chance I get.

Forgiveness is a word often used in Christian circles but often misunderstood. We talk about the forgiveness that God offers us at the time of our salvation and about the fact that he removes our sins as far from us as the east is from the west (Psalm 103:12). We often talk about forgiving others, and we pray about forgiveness whenever we recite the Lord's Prayer: "forgive us our debts, as we also have forgiven our debtors" (Matthew 6:12). And yet, as much as we talk about forgiveness, it is shocking to me how little we actually know about it and how infrequently we apply the practice in our daily lives.

People have many false beliefs and practices associated with the concept of forgiveness. Sometimes we think the only thing that is needed when we sin against someone else is to say "I'm sorry." We expect this phrase to magically wipe away any offense and get us off the hook for any consequence, relational or otherwise. The problem with apologizing like this is that it is too vague, and it tends to deflect culpability and minimize the impact of our actions. Usually "I'm sorry" just means "I feel bad." But what do you feel bad about? Do you feel bad that you were caught? Do you feel bad about what you did? Do you feel bad because the person you sinned against feels bad? To the one hearing those words they can seem cheap, meaningless, insincere, and self-focused. This kind of apology doesn't deal with the wrong done. It often communicates that the primary desire of the one making the apology is to have his bad feelings removed. It is not about the person they sinned against. It is not about God or doing what is right. It is all about self. True forgiveness involves the confession we described in the previous chapter, along with significant requests, and meaningful promises.

On the flip side, when someone says "I'm sorry" to us, we often feel pressured to say "I forgive you" right away because, after all, we are commanded to forgive (Ephesians 4:32), and there are dire warnings in Scripture about not forgiving (Matthew 18:35). This rush to forgiveness also tends to minimize the gravity of the sin committed and the impact it has on the relationships involved. It typically adds further injury to the person who is hurting deeply.

Sometimes we err because we think we don't need to address the sin committed against us. We think all we need to do is "forgive from the heart" (Matthew 18:35). But that concept of forgiveness ignores the clear instruction given earlier in the same passage, that we are supposed to go to someone who has sinned against us and talk about it (Matthew 18:15). It also raises some important questions, such as, what does it mean to forgive from the heart? Or the more fundamental question, what is forgiveness?

Consider this scenario: You come home late from work, without calling, again. As you walk into the house, there is silence. You can feel the boiling heat or icy coldness in the atmosphere of your home (depending on your wife's normal response to frustration). Dare you say anything? Dare you not say anything? "Is everything alright, dear?" you ask, knowing full well that she is upset because you are late. "I'm fine," she replies in that tone she uses to communicate that she is anything but fine. In your bitterness, you just move on, unwilling to acknowledge your lateness and stewing in your own mind about how hard your job is and how she could never understand because she just stays home all day. You had a really important project to work on, but she doesn't care to understand anything about what you do. As the night creeps along, tensions build. Dinner is a silent meal that would make a gathering of monks seem like a bunch of chatty high school girls. After dinner, while you are clearing your place, you spill some sauce on the floor, and the tense silence is shattered.

"You are such a careless slob!" she jabs.

"Oh, get off it! It was an accident!" you fire back.

"If it only happened every once in a while, then it would be an accident. But you spill stuff all the time!"

"I said get off my case. It was an accident. I didn't mean to do it."

"Oh sure, just like you didn't mean to come home late and spoil our evening."

"Hey! What's that supposed to mean? I thought you said you were fine when I came home today. I was late because I was working on an important project. But you don't want to know anything about that. You have no idea what kind of pressure I'm under all the time. You just stay at home all day and do whatever you want!" As you say these words, you begin to regret it, but you are still fired up about being chewed out for some silly nonsense.

"Is that what you think? You think I want to be stuck here in this @*&%$ hole of a house all day doing your laundry and cleaning up after your sorry *&$? All you care about is that &*^%#@! job." As these sentences fly, any regret you had over your words is blanched away by the blood boiling in your veins. You storm out of the room, afraid of what you might say or do if you stayed there.

Later that night, while you are getting ready for bed, things have cooled off and you and your wife decide to make amends. The conversation that ensues will show whether or not you understand biblical forgiveness. For most people the conversation goes something like this: "Honey, I'm really sorry about what I said earlier. I didn't mean those things I said."

"Don't worry about it, sweetie. It's no big deal. I was tired, you were frustrated. We both said things we didn't really mean. Let's just forget about it and go to bed."

The problem with this conversation is that it has nothing to do with forgiveness, because it does not deal with the real sins that took place. You probably know from experience that this kind of conversation also does not resolve the issue or allow the two of you to move forward and toward one another. It is likely to simmer under the surface until the next time something explodes; then it's going to come flying out as ammunition in the next battle.

It would be impossible to fully answer all the questions some-one might have related to forgiveness in this book, let alone in this chapter. For now, I will focus on some key elements that are necessary for you and your wife to understand in your current circumstance. For what follows, I'm deeply indebted to David Powlison, who offered an excellent and succinct discussion of forgiveness in his powerful book, *Good and Angry*.[1]

Two-Factored Forgiveness

When the Bible discusses forgiveness, it describes two aspects of forgiveness: attitudinal forgiveness and transactional forgive-ness. Often, confusion arises because someone is focused on one aspect or the other, or they might be completely unaware of these two components. It is important that you and your wife under-stand both; this is essential for all interrelational sins, not only for your current struggle with pornography.

Attitudinal Forgiveness

The first form of forgiveness is attitudinal forgiveness. This is what the Bible describes as "forgiveness from the heart" (Matthew 18:35). Attitudinal forgiveness refers to the verti-cal aspect of forgiveness where you take the wrongs committed against you and lay them before God. You relinquish any bitter-ness you may have over the hurt, and you ask God to help you in the process. Jesus instructs his followers, including you and me, to make forgiveness of others an important part of our prayers. In Mark 11:25 he teaches, "And whenever you stand praying, forgive, if you have anything against anyone, so that your Father also who is in heaven may forgive you your trespasses."

Attitudinal forgiveness starts with you and God. It isn't as much about the other person at this point as it is about you. Are you truly prepared to forgive? Are you willing to set aside a debt owed to you? Are you internally, at a heart level, ready to forgive?

Going before God with hurts and sins that have been committed against us should remind us of the forgiveness that we have received from him. Multiple times, the Scriptures remind us that our forgiveness of others is motivated by, empowered by, and preceded by the example of forgiveness that God has shown us (Matthew 6:12; Ephesians 4:32; Colossians 3:13). It also reminds us that the debt we are releasing someone else from is far smaller than the debt that God has forgiven on our behalf (Matthew 18:23–35). Attitudinal forgiveness starts with God, but it leads to a heart that is softened toward the offender and ready to offer forgiveness to the repentant sinner.

When you have a full-disclosure conversation with your wife, you want to give her space and time to address this level of forgiveness before rushing on to the second form of forgiveness. She needs time to wrestle with God about what you have done. She needs time for him to soften her heart toward you. *How much time will she need?* you might be wondering. I wish I could tell you, but each situation is different. It is going to depend on your wife, her relationship with you, her unique background, and her understanding of and experience with forgiveness. It is going to depend on the extent of your sin and how it was disclosed to her. It is going to depend on how often you have been down this road before. Most of all, it will depend on God and his work in your heart and your wife's heart. Attitudinal forgiveness means that you are prepared to forgive the other party involved, but you haven't fully forgiven them until you move to the next kind of forgiveness: transactional forgiveness.

Transactional Forgiveness

Attitudinal forgiveness prepares the heart of someone who has been offended to move toward the offender with the offer of transactional forgiveness. Transactional forgiveness is the cancellation of a debt owed. The person to whom the debt is owed chooses to release the violator from the debt. In transactional forgiveness, the party that was sinned against absorbs the debt of the person who sinned against them. They don't exact any penalties for the offense. It is washed away. One way to think about transactional forgiveness is to recognize that it includes the following four promises:

1. I am not going to bring your sin up to anyone else in a harmful way.
2. I am not going to bring the sin up to you again in a harmful way.
3. I am not going to bring this sin up to myself in a harmful way or allow myself to sinfully dwell on it if it comes to mind.
4. I'm not going to allow the sin to stand in the way of our relationship. I choose to move toward you, not away from you, in spite of your sin.

These are hard promises to make and even harder promises to keep. That is why the old adage says, "To err is human; to forgive is divine." The one who can agree to this kind of transaction has to be motivated by and equipped with God's forgiving love. They must have attitudinal forgiveness first.

You may have noticed that the first three promises came with the conditional statement "in a harmful way." The reason for this is simple. There are times when bringing up someone's past sin is the loving thing to do. Let's say you have a child who sins by punching you. Then they ask forgiveness, and you grant it. Next week they do it again, and you repeat the cycle. Let's say this weekly occurrence has continued for a couple of months. Would it be unloving to bring up the past occurrences of punching to your child to help him understand his struggle, what is motivating it, and how to overcome it? Of course the answer is no; it would be loving to bring up those past occurrences. If you are motivated to help someone grow, you can and should bring up past occurrences of forgiven sin as information to use in helping them overcome sinful patterns.

Similarly, there are times when it becomes necessary to discuss someone's past, already forgiven sins with another person. In your own situation, it may be necessary, helpful, and loving for your wife to bring up past instances of pornography use to an accountability ally to help him understand your struggle better. This will likely hurt, but if it is genuinely motivated by love for you and a desire to help you grow, then you need to embrace it, thank God for it, and thank your wife. Don't allow these conversations about the past to mire you down in undue guilt or shame or to become a source of bitterness between you and your wife. Her willingness to discuss this painful history is not evidence of a lack of forgiveness, but an attempt to help you grow.

It can be helpful for your wife to think about your sin if it draws her closer to you and to the Lord. Thoughts about your sin that lead her to loving concern for you, that will encourage and embolden her to fight with you against your sin, can be helpful. She can also reflect on your sin in ways that cause her to praise God for the work he has done to conquer sin and the work he has wrought in you as you grow and transform to be more like Christ. Of course, she must guard her heart carefully and actively seek to put off thoughts of your sin that lead her to bitterness, which will drive a wedge between you and her.

Transactional forgiveness can be initiated by either the offended or the offending party. Jesus tells us that in either situation, whether we remember sin that we have committed against someone else or sin that someone has committed against us, thinking about the sin should drive us to initiate the conversation (Matthew 5:23–25; 18:15). If sin on anyone's part—either yours or someone else's—keeps coming to your mind, then it needs to be dealt with. And because you are thinking about it, you should initiate it.

If you are the person who has been sinned against, you need to go to God and prepare your heart with attitudinal forgiveness so that you are ready to offer transactional forgiveness *if* the offending party asks for it. Notice the emphasis on *if* the offending party asks for forgiveness. You can't actually forgive someone transactionally unless they are willing to receive it. Remember when I said that the word *confession* is rooted in the idea of coming to an agreement on something? If you confront someone over sin and tell them you are ready to forgive them, but they don't think they have actually sinned, then that conversation is not going very far.

Remember the fight I described earlier between you and your wife? What if you tried to address her sinful speech when she swore at you and she said, "I don't know what you are talking about. I didn't use any foul language." She is not going to take forgiveness from you because she doesn't think she needs it.

On the other hand, if she says, "You are right, what I said was sinful and hurtful. It did not honor God and it was unloving to you. Will you please forgive me?" She is standing with open hands ready to receive forgiveness, so you can offer it and thereby release her of the relational debt and make the promises mentioned above. That is transactional forgiveness.

Toward the end of the conversation where you offer a full disclosure of your sin, let her know that you want to ask for forgiveness but you are going to give her time to process what you have shared. Tell her you don't want to rush her to forgiveness. Then ask her to let you know when she is ready to offer transactional forgiveness. You both will continue to meet with your individual biblical counselors and maybe have some meetings together in the interim. She will likely spend some time with her biblical counselor working toward attitudinal forgiveness and resting in God's grace. If you begin to feel impatient with her and wonder if/when she will ever forgive you, pray and ask God to give you patience, reflect on the depth of your sin, consider the pain she is feeling and the hurt she is wrestling through, and talk to your biblical counselor about it. Your biblical counselor should be in dialogue with your wife's biblical counselor about the process. Allow them to address this issue with her. You should not pressure her for forgiveness. That will only compound her hurt and complicate the issue. If she is being disobedient or rebellious toward God by digging her heels in and refusing to forgive, her biblical counselor should be the one to confront her about that.

The forgiveness conversation should not be limited to your pornography use. It should become common in your relationships because sin is common in all your relationships. It is still wise to initiate the conversation either by pointing out sin or confessing sin and allowing time for someone to process the impact of the sin before asking for forgiveness. The amount of time given prior to asking for forgiveness often correlates to the severity of the sin. If you snap at your wife, you can confess that and ask for forgiveness immediately. More serious sins will take longer. After confessing your sin, you can always say something like this: "I know my sin has hurt you. I want to ask you for forgiveness, but I realize you need time to process what I've just told you and to prepare your heart to offer forgiveness. Please let me know when you are ready to forgive." You can also add, "If I haven't heard from you in a week (or insert some other time frame) I'll ask again to see if you have any other questions. I don't want to pester you, but I also value our relationship and don't want to allow the division caused by my sin to grow." This will become easier as both of you grow more practiced in biblical forgiveness.

Forgiveness and Consequences

While transactional forgiveness eliminates the debt of the sinner owed to the one sinned against, it does not mean that there will be no consequences for the sin. For instance, someone who is enslaved to gambling may need to be limited in the amount of money they have access to. This could seem punitive, and in some cases it is (when the spouse who has been sinned against hasn't truly forgiven). But when it is done out of love for the individual and to protect their family, it is a consequence tied to divine discipline (Hebrews 12:5–11), not a punishment. Proper discipline is designed to correct and train, not exact revenge.

There may be consequences for your pornography use—like measures put in place to help prevent further sin in this area—that may tempt you to believe your spouse hasn't truly forgiven you. For instance, it would be wise for your wife to have access to your phone and have a security password that prevents you from adding apps or changing content settings. This can feel like a punishment, but understood correctly it is an act of love intended to help you fight your sin. It is important that you maintain open, honest communication about that with your spouse and biblical counselor. You must consistently remind yourself that these measures are expressions of God's love for you and your spouse's love for you, not attempts to exact revenge or penance for your sin. Your wife also needs to continue to examine her heart to be sure she is walking in genuine forgiveness by keeping the promises she made to you in her transactional forgiveness of your sin.

Reconciliation

Sin separates. When we sin, our relationships are torn apart. Reconciliation brings those relationships back together. Confession and forgiveness are steps in that process, but they are not the end goal. After you have asked forgiveness, your wife has graciously offered it, and you have received it, you must continue to move toward one another. Another fruit of repentance is reconciliation. The best way to do this is for you both to individually and mutually move toward Christ.

It can be easy for people to say they forgive one another but then remain separated by the sin that took place. Reconciliation is a restoration of the relationship. It brings people back together and can make the relationship even stronger. You will want to make practical steps to move toward one another in all areas of life. Think about ways you can come together spiritually, emotionally, intellectually, and physically. Talk with one another. Have regular times for meaningful conversation. Yes, you will need to talk about the kids, schedules, and the normal logistics of life, but don't stop there. Ask about each other's spiritual walk, dreams, and desires. Care for one another in your hurts and losses. Rejoice with each other in your victories and celebrations. Do a Bible study together. Go for walks. Watch movies together. Find activities you can do as a family. Start dating again.

When it comes to your sexual relationship, you may need to refrain from sex for a season after your wife discovers or you disclose pornography use. She is going to feel betrayed and alienated from you sexually and will likely not want to engage with you in that way. You need to allow time for her heart to soften toward you and be willing to invite you back into that intimate relationship.

Your pornography use betrays a heart of selfishness in your sexuality. You need to have a change of heart regarding sex. You need to come to understand sex as an act of love and mutual giving, not merely getting. Rushing your spouse to reengage sexually communicates to her that you are more concerned about your sexual appetite than the pain she is experiencing. I cannot give specific advice on time frames here, but a wise spiritual mentor can help you navigate that question with your wife.

Reconciliation occurs over time as you rebuild love and trust with one another by living life together. Be patient, be persistent. Reconciliation takes time and effort, and Jesus needs to be central in the process.

Remember that your wife is not Jesus. While she is called to forgive like him and is empowered to forgive by him, she is not him. It may take her quite a bit of time, and there will likely be missteps in her forgiveness. Be patient with her, not demanding, not rushing, and not quick to condemn. Your patience with her may involve forgiving her for sins she commits against you in this process. She may say sinful things to you, or she may wrestle with a sinful unwillingness to forgive. These circumstances present opportunities for you to learn and exemplify Christ's forgiveness.

Understanding God's forgiveness of us in Christ is the key motivation for forgiveness between God's children. It is also a key motivation for growing in our love and worship of Christ. As you think on his forgiveness and the forgiveness that he has made possible in your marriage, praise him for it, pray to him and thank him for it. The next chapter will seek to strengthen your growing love for Jesus and show more ways in which you can admire him.

Questions for Action, Discussion, and Reflection

1. How have you dealt with conflict or sin in your marriage in the past?

2. How did those past approaches differ from what has been outlined in this chapter? What changes do you want to make in how you ask for or offer forgiveness?

3. Are there any unresolved conflicts or sins in your life (those you have committed or those committed against you)? If so, write them down. Ask your biblical counselor or mentor to help you devise a transformation plan to pursue forgiveness for these unresolved sins.

Further Reading

Jones, Robert D. *Pursuing Peace: A Christian Guide to Handling Our Conflicts.* Wheaton, IL: Crossway, 2012.

Powlison, David. *Good and Angry: Redeeming Anger, Irritation, Complaining, and Bitterness.* Greensboro, NC: New Growth Press, 2016. See especially chapter 7.

Satrom, Hayley. *Forgiveness: Reflecting God's Mercy.* 31-Day Devotionals for Life. Phillipsburg, NJ: P&R Publishing, 2020.

6

Admiration: Worshiping Jesus

IN THE 90s I was a huge basketball fan. It was a great era to love basketball for many reasons, but one reason soared above them all: Michael Jordan. Now, I have to admit that because I lived in Arizona, I was a Phoenix Suns fan. When Charles Barkley and the Suns faced off against Jordan and the Bulls, I was decked out in purple and orange, Charles Barkley tie and all. Despite this, I believe that Michael Jordan is the best basketball player to ever take the court. And he was more than a basketball player—he became an international icon. The silhouette of his head was identifiable to most people across the globe, and shoes bearing his name and the image of him flying through the air are still popular more than 30 years later. In his prime, everyone not only wanted to know Michael Jordan, we all wanted to be like Mike. This kind of devotion and appreciation is what I call admiration.

As much as we might admire a sports star or some celebrity, our devotion for those figures should pale in comparison to our admiration of Christ. The very purpose of our life is to worship and admire Christ (Romans 11:36). We should want to know him, become like him, and draw others into a relationship with him as well. The central point of life is Jesus. In this chapter, I'm going to talk about how admiration helps us repent and battle our desire for pornography. However, we must remember that Jesus is not just a means to our ends; he is the end, in and of himself. Repentance is a side benefit of knowing him and growing in admiration for him.

The first A in the AAA of fighting sin is admiration. Repentance is a U-turn of our hearts that results in a U-turn of our lives. That means we are heading in a new direction, but we need to not merely turn away from one thing, we need something—or rather someone—to turn to. Admiration is the practice and process of growing our love and appreciation for Christ. At its core, sin is a worship problem. God created humanity as worshipers. We ultimately either worship God, as he intended, or we worship ourselves. Turning from sin in genuine repentance means we turn from worshiping ourselves to worshiping God. Before we came to Christ in saving faith, we lived a life of self-worship. When we turn away from self-worship, we must turn toward Christ and worship him alone. This is a lifelong journey. None of us will fully achieve true, pure worship in this life. But as we journey down this road with Jesus, we will learn more about him while he shapes our desires to be like his and inclines our affections toward him.

Admiration is the key A to genuine repentance—without a growing love for Christ, our hearts may not actually be changed. Amputation and accountability without admiration is merely behavior modification. We don't want to simply change our behavior; we want to gain truly transformed lives. True transformation depends on heart change, and heart change only happens when our thoughts, emotions, and will are transformed by Christ to be like Christ. Therefore, we must get to know him so we can be like him, and then we will live for him.

Drawing Near to Jesus

From 1 John 3:2 "we know that when he appears we shall be like him, because we shall see him as he is." This verse shows us that there is a connection between seeing Jesus, understanding what he is like, and becoming more like him. And, as this verse shows us, this process will not end in this lifetime. The end of this process culminates in us seeing Jesus face-to-face. But the process has already begun in you if you are a Christian. The term *Christian* means "Christlike ones." When we come to saving faith in Jesus, we begin the process of becoming more and more like him. The ultimate purpose of everything that happens in our lives is to glorify God as we are transformed into the image of his only begotten son (Romans 8:28–29).

Have you ever noticed how married couples often gradually begin to look more and more alike as they age? Sometimes the transformation is in obvious things, like dress. Perhaps one spouse begins to do all the clothes shopping and his or her style takes over both wardrobes, or maybe their tastes gradually meld. Whatever it is, people who have been married for a long time tend to dress alike. There are also other, more subtle, transformations, such as patterns of speech and mannerisms. Time spent together changes people. We conform to and transform those we spend time with. Proximity breeds conformity. That principle is true for our relationship with Jesus as well. The more time we spend with him, the more we will come to know him, and the more we will become like him.

So how do we spend time with Jesus? God has designed several activities to help us draw closer to him. If you have been a Christian for any amount of time you are likely familiar with them. We call them habits of holiness, spiritual disciplines, means of grace, etc. They include prayer, Bible reading/study, church attendance, Scripture meditation/memorization, fasting, etc. I am not going to describe the details of these practices, for there are plenty of other great books on this topic. I'll recommend a few books at the end of this chapter. I encourage you to pick at least one and read it after you finish this book, or alongside it, if this is an area you want to immediately begin working on. If you are reading this book in conjunction with counseling, then the counselor likely has already helped you grow in practicing some spiritual disciplines. If your counselor hasn't, I encourage you to find a solid biblical counselor who will incorporate these ordinary means of grace into your counseling experience and life beyond.

Some people think that only very religious or spiritual people practice spiritual disciplines, but that is not the case. Practicing spiritual disciplines cannot be compared to the extra hours of weight lifting and conditioning that bodybuilders and elite athletes perform. Instead, Bible reading, prayer, corporate worship, etc. are more akin to eating, breathing, and drinking. They are not extra things that will take normal spiritual health to new and extreme heights; they are the bare essentials that keep us spiritually alive and growing. You cannot expect to have a thriving spiritual life if you are starving your soul. You cannot overcome sexual sin, one manifestation of the battle between the spirit and the flesh (Galatians 5:16–17), if you are starving the spirit and feeding the flesh.

You can't truly grow your relationship with Jesus if you aren't spending time with him. As I mentioned before, you can spend time with Jesus in a variety of ways and times. You can schedule intentional, personal time together (daily prayer/Bible reading time), you can have more casual interactions throughout the day (prayers and meditations), and you can hang out with him in group settings (Bible studies, small groups, and corporate gatherings of the local church).

The reality is that Jesus is with you all day, every day. You don't need to invite him along for the ride; he is there. You simply have to take notice. Have you ever been ignored? Have you ever ignored anyone? It is a really strange and uncomfortable phenomenon to be physically present with someone who is mentally absent. Sometimes we ignore people intentionally. We ignore people when they make us uncomfortable, when we are frustrated with them, when we see them as a distraction to what we want to do, and for a host of other reasons. If we step back and look at these situations from the outside, they are almost always completely foolish. When we ignore someone, we are acting like they don't exist. This can demonstrate a swath of things about us, none of them appealing. On the "innocent" end of the spectrum, we are completely oblivious to reality; near the middle of the spectrum, we are neglecting the people around us; and on the more insidious end of the spectrum, we are communicating that we wish the other person didn't exist, maybe even that we wish they were dead. Where are you on this spectrum as it relates to Jesus? Do you wish he didn't exist so you could do all the sinful things you want to do without any consequence? Are you avoiding him? Are you simply neglecting him? Or are you completely oblivious to his existence? The question is not whether or not he is doing his part. He is there. He is walking with you. The question is whether you are going to pay attention to him.

The Bible has many descriptions of Jesus's relationship with you as an individual and a part of his church. You are part of a body of which he is the head (Ephesians 1:22–23; 5:23; Colossians 1:18). He is described as a vine that gives life to you as one of its branches (John 15:4–5). He is a bridegroom that protects, provides for, and prepares a home for his bride, the church (Ephesians 5:25–33).

Meditate on his character, his actions, his life, and his relationship with you. Read the gospels (Matthew, Mark, Luke, and John) to see him in action. Learn about him and get to know how he lives, acts, treats people, and spends time with his Heavenly Father. See how much he cares for people, including you. Read Ephesians chapters 1 and 5, Colossians 1, and John 15, and think about how he relates to you and you relate to him. Think about the cross and what he did to save you from sin. Think about the resurrection. Watch movies that depict his life in memorable ways that put flesh on him. Listen to and sing along with songs that draw your attention to his wonders and wonderful nature. Find your own unique ways of connecting with Jesus. Maybe for you it is going for a hike in the mountains. Maybe you meet with him while fly-fishing in a quiet stream. Maybe writing a poem, painting, drawing, or carving something creative connects you to your creator. Maybe it is fellowshipping around a campfire with good friends. Whatever it is, find ways to connect with Jesus. Find righteous pleasures that exhilarate you and leave you in awe of our God. Enjoy experiences that bring you peace, calm, and stillness as you sit and commune with your Savior.

Enjoy his blessings and thank him for them. When you eat a great steak, praise God. When you go for a hike in his artful creation, take note of it and talk to him about what you are thinking, feeling, etc. Thank him for the glorious gift of creation. When you have amazing sex with your wife, praise God! Thank him for that delightful act of worshipful intimacy he designed.

Living for His Glory

As you get to know Jesus and draw closer to him, you should also grow in your desire to live for him. Romans 11:36 says, "For from him and through him and to him are all things. To him be glory forever." The ultimate purpose of every person is to bring glory to God. Bringing God glory simply means revealing more of him to ourselves and others so that we see him more clearly, understand and appreciate him more fully, and worship him as a result. We accomplish this most by becoming more like Jesus. As I described earlier, the process of sanctification is like putting that broken statue back together. The longer we are walking with Jesus, the more we will look like him. The more of him we will see in ourselves, and the more people will see him in us. As you move forward in this process, you will grow in gratitude for what he has done for you, and you will praise him for what he has done and who he is. Others will see changes in you. Those closest to you will notice the changes most, but even those who know you more distantly will see subtle changes. As your sin infected and affected all your relationships, your sanctification can influence them all to glorify God. Everything we have, everything we are, and everything we can hope to be are tied up in him. All of you should be all for him.

Questions for Action, Discussion, and Reflection

1. How would you describe your current relationship with Jesus? What are your primary thoughts, desires, and feelings toward him?

2. When do you feel most connected to Christ? How do you express your love and care for him?

3. What does your current practice of spiritual disciplines look like? If you don't practice spiritual disciplines regularly or know you are particularly weak in one (or more) areas, make a transformation plan with the help of a spiritual mentor to grow in exercising these means of grace. Write your plans down and begin implementing them.

4. What other activities do you engage in that draw you closer to God? What things do you do that inspire you to praise him?

Further Reading

Ortlund, Dane Calvin. *Gentle and Lowly: The Heart of Christ for Sinners and Sufferers*. Wheaton: Crossway, 2020.

Solomon, Curtis. *Transformation Bible Study Journal*. Available at solomonsoulcare.com.

Whitney, Donald S. *Spiritual Disciplines for the Christian Life*. Colorado Springs: NavPress, 1997.

7

Accountability

"NO ONE FIGHTS alone" is the slogan of a ministry I work with that helps veterans overcome their battle with post-traumatic stress.[1] They realize the divine truth that "It is not good that the man should be alone" (Genesis 2:18). Walking through life alone is foolishness even in the best of times. It is downright dangerous when we are facing trials and temptations (Ecclesiastes 4:7–12). Isolation is a tactic used by every enemy from the pride of lions chasing down a zebra, to enemy combatants in Afghanistan, to Satan, the greatest enemy of all. If our enemies can get us alone, we are dead meat. This is why we need the second A in the AAA way to fight sin: accountability. Accountability necessarily involves other people. When we bring other people onto our team, into our fight with pornography, we are far more likely to win the battle.

You *Need* Accountability

Satan will try all kinds of tactics to keep you by yourself in your fight against porn. He will try to convince you that no one else struggles like you do. This can lead to shame over our sin, which then fosters silence. In a weird, twisted way, that lie can also lead to a form of pride that says, "No one can offer me help because no one has struggled like I have." You must battle that lie with the truth of God's Word from 1 Corinthians 10:13, which says, "No temptation has overtaken you that is not common to man. God is faithful, and he will not let you be tempted beyond your ability, but with the temptation he will also provide the way of escape, that you may be able to endure it." You have read my words telling you that I've struggled with porn. Sixty-four percent of Christian men say they use porn once a month, and one in five youth pastors and one of every seven senior pastors say they currently struggle with porn.[2] Now you've heard it from God himself; you are not alone—this struggle is a common problem. Allow the truth that you are not alone to drive you toward others to find help and support one another in this battle.

Another lie we are tempted to believe is that we can hide our sin. The Bible is very clear: "your sin will find you out" (Numbers 32:23). Hidden sin is like a cancerous tumor. Left unchecked, it doesn't go way; instead, it grows and spreads until it kills. While your wife and friends may not know for sure that you are viewing pornography, your sin is impacting those relationships, and it will eventually come out. God loves his children too much to allow their sin to remain hidden. Rather than allowing it to grow in secret until it is discovered, or until it destroys your life, expose it. Shine light on it. Tell someone about your struggle and get help to remove it from your life.

Perhaps the worst lie we are told is that we can handle this sin on our own. You probably know this firsthand, although you may be trying to convince yourself otherwise. You cannot fight off pornography on your own. You've tried. You may even have had seasons of success, but inevitably you turn back and give into your craving for illicit images. You can't do it on your own. You need others in your life who can help you bear this burden, help you fight sin, and help spur you on to love and good deeds (Galatians 6:1–2; Hebrews 10:24–25). Accountability will have many forms and come in many ways, but, for now, the primary truth you need to grasp is that you must enlist help in your battle against pornography. You can't do it alone. No one fights alone!

In the last chapter, we learned about the necessity and centrality of our relationship with Jesus. Christ is the only ally you need in an ultimate sense, and he is the primary one you should rely on. If you were trapped in a cave, or let's say in isolation caused by quarantine during a global pandemic, Jesus can help you avoid pornography. Thankfully, however, he has chosen to bless you with other allies—most importantly your wife (we will discuss her role in the next chapter), as well as brothers to build you up and support you in this fight. Before you build your transformation team, it is important to understand what accountability is and what roles you need your team members to play.

Defining Accountability

Galatians 6:1–2 says, "Brothers, if anyone is caught in any transgression, you who are spiritual should restore him in a spirit of gentleness. Keep watch on yourself, lest you too be tempted. Bear one another's burdens, and so fulfill the law of Christ."

Accountability is a God-given aid to help us forsake sin and put on righteousness. At its core, accountability involves relationships that help us accept responsibility for our actions (including the consequences), learn from past behaviors, find ways to put off sin, and encourage righteous living in place of sinning. Accountability is most often experienced as one component of true Christian friendship where brothers and sisters in Christ "stir up one another to love and good works" (Hebrews 10:24). It can also come in the form of Christians we sinned against coming to us to address that sin (Matthew 18:15). It may include other witnesses accompanying the brother or sister we have sinned against, to urge us to repent if we refuse to turn from our sin after their initial conversation (Matthew 18:16–20). On occasion, God intervenes in direct and explicit ways to cause his followers to turn from sin and toward righteousness. One example is God sending the prophet Nathan to confront David over his sexual predation of Bathsheba and subsequent murder of Uriah (2 Samuel 12). All these forms of accountability point to the ultimate reality that we will give an account of our lives before God (Romans 14:12; 2 Corinthians 5:10). However, since this final judgment does not include any fear of condemnation or punishment for Christians (Romans 8:1), fear of judgment should not be our primary motivation for overcoming sin here in this life. Furthermore, accountability that uses fear of man as a primary tool for motivating repentance and righteousness also misses the mark. That is one key factor behind faulty accountability. Before we discuss more about proper accountability, it will be helpful for us to examine what accountability is not.

What Accountability Is Not

One common argument against accountability comes from people who say, "I've tried accountability in the past. It doesn't work." The ubiquity of this experience does not validate the rejection of accountability. If you did a broad survey of people on the effectiveness of prayer, many would argue that it "doesn't work," but that does not mean prayer is actually ineffective, nor does it lead us to abandon the practice. Hopefully, I have established a solid biblical argument for the necessity of accountability, but we will examine some more thoughts that help us understand faulty applications of accountability and why they "don't work."

First, we need to understand what we mean by accountability "working." Do we expect that accountability will magically take away the desire to look at pornography? Then of course accountability doesn't work. That is not what it is intended to do. If you are looking for some magic bullet that will instantaneously remove your sinful, sexual lusts, you will be disappointed. You can pray for this, and God may grant that request, but as I've said before, that is not the way God usually works in the lives of believers.

Accountability is also not simply a list of questions one person asks another to uncover sinful behavior. Many who "tried accountability" in the 1990s and early 2000s treated accountability this way. Men met regularly, often weekly, and would simply ask each other a list of questions about their experiences with lust or porn during the past week. This form of "accountability" fails for a variety of reasons. For one thing, they falter because the primary motivation for change is fear of man, not fear of God. In these programs, men are being motivated to remain pure so that they won't have to report failure to their accountability partners. Another related reason that they fail is their emphasis on avoiding the negative sin. Most of the questions used in this approach only dig into whether or not there was participation in sexual sin. They focus on what should be put off without any instruction on how or what to put on in its place. Proper accountability does discourage you from pursuing sin, but it also equips you to move forward in righteousness.

Accountability is also not a regular meeting to commiserate with fellow sinners. One of the common pitfalls of accountability relationships is that men don't call each other to account. One guy opens up and shares how he looked at porn that week and then a few other guys share similar experiences. They pat each other on the back and thank each other for being honest and feel better that they are not alone in their sin. Misery loves company. There is truth in this statement, and there is a hint of truth in the idea of gathering people who struggle with the same sin to discuss their struggle with that particular sin. It puts flesh on the idea that our temptations are common to man (1 Corinthians 10:13). Experientially, most of us will testify that there is some value and mutual understanding gained through sharing our experiences with others and hearing about theirs. But the Scriptures don't jump from the idea that our temptations are common to man to saying that the practical implication is that groups of people should gather based on their shared temptation and sin. The verse quoted at the beginning of this chapter points to the fact that those who are "caught in any transgression" are to be helped by those who are "spiritual"

(Galatians 6:1). Those who are spiritual are not some elite group of Christians; rather, they are believers who are still prone to temptation (Galatians 6:1) but they are currently walking by the Spirit (Galatians 5:25). The regular pattern of their lives is characterized more by the fruit of the Spirit (Galatians 5:22–23) than the works of the flesh (Galatians 5:19–21). Those whose lives have become entangled with or characterized by works of the flesh shouldn't rely on others in the same position, but on Christ and those who are walking by his Spirit.

I do not want to discourage you if you have found help through pornography accountability groups. I know many men who have been helped by these groups. But I also know many who have not been helped, and some who have gone deeper into sexual sin because of things they learned from others in these groups. Those that have the most benefit are run well by godly men who have seen great sanctification in this area and know how to lead productive conversations, not mere commiseration. A good facilitator will encourage open honest confession, but also enforce consequences outlined in transformation plans and point people to righteous replacements. The comfort that comes from knowing you are not alone in your sin is not meant to make you feel comfortable with your sin but to empower you with hope that change and growth are possible. The primary problem with sin-centered accountability groups is that Scripture points to a different kind of accountability relationship as the way we should engage our sinful tendencies.

Some accountability relationships have failed due to the failings on the part of the person who struggles with porn, or the person/people invited to give accountability, or both. What are some common problems in the accountability relationship?

The primary problem in an accountability relationship stems from the failure to be fully honest, open, and transparent. This can result when the person who struggles fails to speak the truth, the whole truth, and nothing but the truth regarding their sexual sin and temptation. There are a plethora of reasons for this so we can't tackle them all. Suffice it to say that if you were not fully honest in your past accountability relationships, then you can't blame the accountability relationship for the failure; you need to take responsibility yourself.

A second related problem is a failure on the part of the person providing accountability to draw out the truth. People who struggle with porn are usually good liars. That includes outright lies, half-truths, twisting words, etc. Someone who is offering accountability needs to be creative and direct when asking another about their sexual temptation. You can't simply say, "How's it going?" or "How's it been this past week?" The person struggling with porn can easily dodge those kinds of questions with an honest answer because they perceive their past week as being "Fine." But that can leave out the lustful lingering looks, musings over past images in their minds, or the three times they visited porn sites on their phone that week. To counteract this problem, accountability partners need to ask multiple times and ask specifically about whether or not they have been fully honest in their retelling. They can be creative in their approach by asking for the same information in different ways. For example, they could ask any of the following questions:

- Have you looked at any porn this week?
- Have you been tempted to lust in your heart this week?
- Has anything inadvertently come across any of your screens or devices that drew you into lustful longing?
- Is there anyone in your life, in images you have seen, or in your imagination that has enticed you toward lust this past week?

Lists of questions can be helpful, but if you only ask the same thing over and over, then it will become easy to anticipate the questions and avoid the truth.

A third problem in an accountability relationship is failure to follow through. In the immediate aftermath of any emergency or crisis, all hands are on deck. But when the crisis phase passes away, so does the urgency that initiated many of the responses, and things settle back to the way they have been. Accountability is often this way. Everyone is on board and committed right after a discovery or disclosure, but as time passes, all parties involved can get lax in their vigilance. After a while, the accountability often goes away completely. Both parties need to be committed to ongoing, long-term vigilance.

The fourth area where accountability groups or relationships often go awry is by exclusively dealing with sexual lust. Your accountability relationships should never focus solely nor even primarily on your porn use. Instead, they should include this aspect of your life, understanding that your life is not only or primarily about porn.

What Accountability Is

So what does effective, biblical accountability look like? *Relationship* is a key word in any accountability relationship. The best accountability is going to come through meaningful friendship with at least one loving, mature Christian with whom you enjoy a genuine relationship. Ideally this relationship will exist within the context of the local church where you are a member. The church is the body of Christ. We are all members of that one body, united in the most significant ways. The most important realities and truths of life unify us. You need someone in your life who believes and holds to the tenets of the Christian faith, who sees you on a regular basis, who knows you and knows God. The relationship does not center on your struggle with sin and temptation (let alone one aspect of your sin); rather, it encompasses all of your life. I like to think of these close friends as allies. They are people who are aligned with you in your mission and goals and who fight alongside you against common enemies.

Porn should not be the only thing you talk about with your ally. You should share other struggles you face, and you should share your joys, strengths, gifts, and growth. You actually don't need to talk about porn every time you communicate, but it should be a regularly recurring topic. The frequency of discussion should increase as the need arises in seasons of greater temptation or struggle. If porn is all you ever discuss, you both will eventually tire of the relationship, let it dwindle, or maybe even actively avoid it. Go deep in your conversations about all aspects of life, have fun together, and build a real friendship. This will keep you close for the long haul and make it easier to discuss your struggle with sins.

Over a lifetime, ally relationships will develop and grow. There may be seasons, like now, where you need to rely heavily on a brother or brothers. But there will likely come times when they need to rely on you as well. Don't neglect being a good listener and ally for your allies. You are not a ministry project; you are a friend, a brother in Christ, an ally in the fight against evil and for good.

Practically speaking, who you have this close relationship with will likely change as well. If you move, you will need to establish new relationships with people in your local church. It can be helpful to maintain contact with someone who has known you for a long time and has walked with you through your struggle with porn. But you will also need at least one person who is in your local vicinity. This person should be someone who can see you interacting with your wife and family on a regular basis. He should be someone who can recognize signs of sin and deception, who can give you a hug and a shoulder to cry on, or a swift kick in the pants (figuratively speaking) when you need it, and someone who can give you a pat on the back or fist pump to celebrate growth and victory. You need both local friends and long-term friends (if you have never moved, these may be the same). As an example, in my life I have one friend I talk to weekly via phone. We were roommates in college, and he has been with me through thick and thin. We've lived in the same location and across the country from each other. He is a constant companion. I also have dear brothers in my local church that I have developed deep relationships with. They know all my struggles and my strengths, and they have the freedom to ask about anything at any time.

Your accountability relationship should be with another man, or a couple of men, who are trustworthy and growing in godliness—men you can be fully honest with and who will be honest with you. Sharing an age or stage of life, some interests, and a sense of humor are all nice, but they are not essential to these types of relationships. Godly character is what matters most, and the ability to communicate wisdom is second in importance. You want someone who walks by the Spirit, which is demonstrated by expressions of love, joy, peace, patience, kindness, goodness, faithfulness, gentleness, and self-control (Galatians 5:22–23). Also, they need to be willing and able to speak the truth in love (Ephesians 4:15). *Part* of your relationship will involve helping you implement your plans for battling pornography. We will discuss some particular steps in Chapter 9. In the next chapter we will also discuss the importance of including your wife in this battle. No one fights alone!

Questions for Action, Discussion, and Reflection

1. Is there anything you are still hiding that would prevent you from pursuing genuine openness and transparency in an accountability relationship?

2. Is there anyone in your life right now who truly knows you and your struggles? If so, who are they? Write their names down. If not, is there anyone in your life that you could begin to pursue that type of relationship with? Establish this relationship ASAP.

Further Reading

Croft, Brian. *Help! He's Struggling With Pornography.* Wapwallo-pen, PA: Shepherd Press, 2010.

Holmes, Jonathan. *The Company We Keep: In Search of Biblical Friendship.* Minneapolis: Cruciform Press, 2014. This book will guide you to make solid, life-long, Christian friendships, which is an essential aspect of all Christian life, including your fight with pornography.

8

Your Wife Is
Your Second Greatest Ally

Read 1 Samuel 25 before you read this chapter.

DURING MY BASIC training, a guy in my unit could never seem to grasp the concept that when you are standing at attention or marching you have to hold your hands with your fingers curled up, not quite a fist but not relaxed either. Our drill instructors would make him hold rocks in his hands while we marched or stood in formation. The unfortunate airman got stuck with the nickname "Box of Rocks" when one of the drill instructors told him he must be "as dumb as a box of rocks" to need a learning aid in order to follow such a simple instruction. Nicknames are common throughout humanity, and they often highlight an outstanding feature of someone—for good or ill. When we get a cool nickname, we usually like it because it highlights one of our positive features. On the other hand, as "Box of Rocks" demonstrates, nicknames can also emphasize some of our less-than-desirable traits.

In 1 Samuel 25, we meet another man who received a nickname tied to an undesirable attribute.[1] What did everyone call this man? *Fool.* In our Bibles we have the name Nabal, which is the English transliteration of the Hebrew word for fool. I don't know about you, but I would not be too happy if everyone I knew, including my wife, was running around calling me Fool, or Stupid, or Idiot. Of course, as with most nicknames, they are not chosen but assigned, and in Nabal's case he had certainly earned the moniker. What was it about Nabal that earned him this name? We can't say for sure how exactly Nabal came to be called fool, but we can see some very clear indications regarding why he earned the nickname in the Bible's account of this man's life.

When we are first introduced to Nabal in 1 Samuel 25, we find out that he was a very rich man who had a beautiful and intelligent wife named Abigail (vv. 2–3). However, we are also told that he was "harsh and badly behaved" (v. 3). Throughout the chapter, Nabal's bad behavior and foolishness are on display. He harshly insulted David and his men and refused to share provisions with them even though they were the ones who had protected and preserved his wealth (vv. 5–11). His insult against David went far deeper than refusal to share food; Nabal questioned David's roots and right to be the ruler of Israel, though David had been anointed as God's chosen king (1 Samuel 16:12–13). In doing this, Nabal not only rejected David's authority, but also the sovereign rule of God. Nabal was so dismissive and oblivious that even when his life and livelihood were being threatened, he held a massive, drunken feast (1 Samuel 25:36). He became so drunk, in fact, that his wife didn't even share how she intervened and saved his life until he sobered up the next day (v. 37).

All of this demonstrates that Nabal deserved his nickname and that he is not someone we should emulate. The passage also highlights one other essential feature of Nabal that makes him a foolish and "worthless" man. In verse seventeen we are told, "he is such a worthless man that one cannot speak to him." Nabal was so arrogant and proud that in spite of his obvious foolishness and moral failings, he refused to listen to anyone. He refused to listen to David, the anointed King of Israel; he refused to listen to his servants; and his wife was so used to being ignored that she didn't even go to him with her plan to rescue the household (v. 19).

When Nabal's servant pleads with Abigail to intervene on behalf of their household, he describes Nabal as a "worthless" man (v. 17). The Hebrew word translated as "worthless" can also be translated as "wickedness" and carries the nuance of "troublemaker, i.e., a person who does evil, so is of little worth."[2] The servant ties Nabal's refusal to listen to anyone to his evil worthlessness.

So you must ask yourself, are you like Nabal in this regard? Do you listen to and accept the counsel of others? Or do you refuse to listen to others when they confront you? What about the counsel, intercessions, pleading, and interventions of your wife? My hope is that you will take two things away from this chapter: (1) accountability is necessary and refusal to utilize it makes you foolish, and (2) your wife should be your second greatest ally in this battle against pornography.

Since your wife is your second greatest ally in this battle, you need to listen to her. She should not only be "allowed" to speak truths (even hard truths) to you, but you should seek her wisdom. Your heart's desire in this fight for purity should not simply be to avoid the sin of pornography and its associated lusts and activities. Your desire should be to pursue righteousness and become like Jesus. In order to do so, you should not just be grudgingly open to accountability, to input from others, but actually crave it and pursue it because you long to use any means of grace that God bestows on us to truly be transformed. Be like David in this instance: recognize and value wisdom and seek it out. Don't be a Nabal and refuse to listen to your wife.

I don't know where you are in relation to the idea that your wife can be one of your most important allies right now. Perhaps you are fully on board because you have a great, honest relationship with your wife. You appreciate and invite her accountability, aid, and insights into your struggle with porn. If so, fantastic! Please send me a message telling me how you got to this point. More than likely that description is not where you are, but I want to hold it out there as a real possibility of where your journey can take you. Most of us who struggle with porn find it challenging to invite our wives into the process and maintain a loving, gracious relationship as we walk in repentance and she walks in forgiveness. In all likelihood, right now you are somewhere between still hiding your sin from your wife and viewing her as the purity police who is always patrolling and prying into your private life. Even worse, you may see her as the enemy who needs to be kept at bay. So how do you get from where you are to where you should be?

First, you must commit to the goal of glorifying God no matter what your wife does. Your response and commitment to this process cannot be dependent upon whether or not she cooperates. The apostle Paul put it this way: "So whether we are at home or away, we make it our aim to please him" (2 Corinthians 5:9). The verse reminds us that no matter what your context, your aim, your goal, your purpose should be to please God. So it doesn't matter if you have a wife who is cooperative, loving, wise, and wonderful or a wife who is harsh, difficult, or foolish, your aim is to please God. Your primary motivation in all of life is God's pleasure. Regardless of whether or not anyone is around, your ambition needs to be to please the Lord.

What if your wife were to leave you today? Would you still be motivated to put aside pornography and pursue purity? You don't have to answer out loud. But you should ponder it. Pray about it. Ask God to give you a heart that hungers and thirsts for righteousness (Matthew 5:6), a heart that yearns to strive for purity no matter what. Even if your wife does commit to the process of being an ally in your fight against pornography, she will never fulfill her roles and responsibilities perfectly, so you need a firm, immovable, foundational goal on which to rebuild your life—to glorify God no matter what. Your primary goal cannot be to save your marriage or to keep your wife happy. These are not bad goals in and of themselves, but they are not sufficient goals to truly transform your life and keep you on the straight and narrow. You can have these goals as complements to your primary goal of glorifying God in all you do. To glorify God means reflecting God more clearly. Making him more known to yourself and others in a way that deepens our worship (quality), increases our worship (quantity), and fosters that worship in others.

Second, resolve in your heart to love your wife and enlist her as your ally in this fight. The reality is that she is more vested in your transformation than any other human walking on the planet. She has more to lose than anyone else if you fall back into pornography, and she has more to gain as you grow. She also has more contact with you than anyone else so she can be more alert to temptation and trouble from without and within you. She can also be more aware of the growth and change in you and can be your greatest supporter and co-celebrator as you continue down this path together.

Becoming allies in this fight is likely going to take a serious shift of thinking on both your parts. I mentioned above the tendency and temptation for wives to become purity police toward their husbands. You can probably relate to this feeling. Most couples hurt by pornography fall into this pattern at some point, and it makes the relationship adversarial. Wives turn into detectives trying to uncover and prosecute secret sins. Husbands are then tempted to take on the role of master criminal, seeking to outwit the detective with new ways of pulling off the crime without getting caught. Another metaphor for the experience is that a wife may feel like a parent trying to control an irresponsible, disobedient, deceitful teen by uncovering and disciplining bad behavior. What couples need is a shift from perceiving one another as adversaries to seeing each other as allies.

Because pornography use hurts your spouse, it can be easy for her to see you as the enemy, and then you respond in kind. But neither of you are the enemy. Sin is the enemy, and you can work together to battle it. When you come to understand your relationship this way, then you will grow in your willingness and desire to have your wife help you in the fight. You go from fighting one another to fighting sin together. Her questions about your struggle are no longer seen as interrogations, but instead as loving concern. The steps she takes to help you fight are not seen as punitive, but loving.

Of course, the relationship will work best if both of you understand your roles in this way, but don't wait for your wife to change her perspective. Take the lead in this. Ask God to help you see your wife as a gift, a co-laborer, an ally in the fight. Then tell your wife about this shift in your thinking. Tell her that you don't want to see her as an enemy, but instead as an ally. Tell her that you appreciate and desire her help in this fight. It might take her (and you) some time to come around to the idea, but your relationship on this matter won't change if you don't start changing. As you move forward, remind yourself when she asks about your struggle that it is for your good. When she follows up about an accountability relationship, remind yourself that she is doing this to fight something you want to fight as well.

The specific ways a wife will provide accountability vary from couple to couple. You will need help in determining the best plan for you and your wife. I recommend enlisting a biblical counselor or mentor couple to help the two of you devise a solid transformation plan that outlines the roles and responsibilities you will each take to fight this battle. Once you come up with a plan, be sure to write it down. I'll discuss more aspects of this written plan in chapter 9. This transformation plan will be shared with all your transformation team. The next section will identify a few general principles that apply to everyone and a few examples of the kinds of details each couple will need to discuss.

General Principles and Details to Discuss

One important general principle is that your wife should not be the only, or even the primary, person you maintain an accountability relationship with. You need at least one godly man who knows your struggle and is in regular contact with you about it. This may sound at odds with the claim that your wife is your second greatest ally in your fight against pornography, so let me explain. Your wife's relationship with you involves accountability, but it is much more than that. She is an ally in this fight in more ways than ensuring you stay accountable to your transformation plan. As a matter of fact, having another man be that frontline/top level accountability person prevents your wife from becoming the purity police in your home. As we just covered, the dynamic of a wife "policing" her husband is a common problem in marriages where the husband struggles with pornography. It adds a great deal of pressure to her and negatively affects the relationship with her husband. Having regular frequent conversations with your accountability ally removes that burden from your wife. She still has the freedom to ask how things are going when she feels the need, but she should not feel the pressure of being the only person asking you about these things.

You should keep your wife informed on how you are doing generally and confess any specific violations of your transformation plan. Your accountability ally should also know about violations to the transformation plan, and he can also keep a closer watch on your temptations and struggle. For instance, my wife and I have agreed that I'll let her know on the third Thursday of every month how things are going, unless there is some violation of our transformation plan agreement. But each week I talk with a friend who knows about my struggle. We talk about a variety of other things, but he regularly asks how I am doing in this area of life. Each couple is different, and you can tailor your plan to your particular needs. The main thing is to find a balance where your wife does not feel like she is alone in this battle, she doesn't feel like she has to be the purity police, but she also doesn't feel cut off from the process.

As you draft your transformation plan, you can also discuss how your wife can aid you in this battle by providing barriers for external temptation. Our plan includes Jenny checking the mail during the months when swimsuit catalogs abound. She also went toe-to-toe with Victoria's Secret for a few months to get us removed from their mailing list. In addition, Jenny maintains the passwords for things that can be a source of temptation, including the password to change privacy and content material on my phone. We have set my phone so that I cannot add apps without her password being entered.

These are just a few general principles and some specific examples that you will need to discuss, discern, and determine together as you move forward in this battle. After reading those details, you might be thinking to yourself, *There is no way I am giving up that kind of privacy and control to anyone!* If you are thinking something along those lines, let me remind you what Nabal's servant said about him: "he is such a worthless man that one cannot speak to him" (1 Samuel 25:17). Part of what got you into the mess that you are in right now is trying to go it alone and neglecting the second greatest ally you have in this fight—your wife. Don't be a Nabal!

While 1 Samuel 25 sets Nabal up as a bad example, it also provides us David as an example to follow. Now David was no innocent man. He was not perfect, and he failed in some major ways—incase you don't remember David's story: he raped a woman and then had her husband murdered in an attempt to cover up his sexual sin. But despite these significant shortcomings, we can still learn from David's response to Abigail in 1 Samuel 25.

When Nabal's servant went to Abigail, beseeching her to intervene so that David and his men wouldn't destroy the entire household of Nabal, she didn't bother to go to Nabal; instead, she went to David. She prepared a gift of provisions for David and his men, and then she rode out to meet them. When she saw them, she dismounted and got on the ground, bowing humbly to David. At that moment Abigail didn't have the hindsight of history that we do. She didn't know what the outcome would be and whether or not David would even slow his horse or just trample her under hoof. She was putting her life on the line in order to protect her family. When David did stop, she accepted responsibility for Nabal's foolish deeds and interceded on behalf of her family and household.

In the midst of her intercession, Abigail wisely and tactfully confronted David and the sinful heart that was driving him to destroy (vv. 26, 28, 31). Read David's amazing response to this wise woman in verses 32–33: "And David said to Abigail, 'Blessed be the LORD, the God of Israel, who sent you this day to meet me! Blessed be your discretion, and blessed be you, who have kept me this day from bloodguilt and from avenging myself with my own hand!'"

Abigail's confrontation of David did not upset him, did not invoke retaliation from him, nor did it cause him to cower back in feelings of self-doubt or shame. Instead, David repented of his sinful intentions, praised God for delivering him from sin by sending Abigail, and thanked Abigail for her wise intervention. As a matter of fact, David regarded Abigail so highly that when Nabal died shortly thereafter, David asked her to be his wife. He wanted a woman by his side who would confront him when he was acting foolishly or stepping out of line with God's will.

How you respond to your wife when she comes to you about your sin says a great deal about you. It reveals a tremendous amount about how you view yourself, her, your sin, and God. It is also an indicator about the direction of your life and what awaits you in the future. Nabal is a very clear example of God's warning that he opposes the proud (Proverbs 3:34; James 4:6; 1 Peter 5:5). Ten days after Abigail informed Nabal about her intervention, the Lord struck him down dead (1 Samuel 25:38). God may not strike you down if you ignore your wife's counsel regarding your pornography use, but the Bible is clear—sexual sin left unchecked leads to all manner of destruction (Proverbs 5:3–4; 9–14; 22–23; 6:25–29; 32–35; 7:22–27; 29:3; 1 Corinthians 6:18).

So what's it going to be? Are you going to be a fool, like Nabal, refusing to listen to the counsel of anyone—including me, others from your church, and your wife? Or are you going to be like David and repent, praise God, and embrace the caring confrontation of those who love you and want your life to be transformed?

A Word about Sex with Your Wife

One unique way that your wife can be your ally in your fight against pornography is through your sexual relationship. This is not the most important way she can help you, but she is the only one who can help you in this way. I'm going to start by clarifying a significant misunderstanding that often comes with this topic and then encourage you to make the most of your sexual union in marriage.

Let me be absolutely clear: Your wife is in no way, shape, or form responsible for your pornography use. Having more sex with her or "better" sex with her is not the solution to your pornography problem. Far too much damage has been inflicted on hurting wives by husbands, counselors, and pastors who say something like "If you just have more sex, your husband won't look at porn." This is a false conclusion drawn from true, *but selective* biblical premises about sex in marriage. Yes, under normal circumstances marriages are supposed to include a regular rhythm of sexual activity (1 Corinthians 7:5). Yes, deprivation of sex in marriage provides Satan an opportunity for temptation (1 Corinthians 7:5). Yes, marital sex is a solution offered by God to help those who are tempted toward sexual immorality (1 Corinthians 7:2). But those truths do not combine to transfer responsibility for a husband's sexual sin onto his wife. Even if a woman was sinfully withholding sex from her husband, it would not justify him turning outside the marriage relationship to satisfy himself sexually. Even when Eve enticed Adam to sin directly, she was not held accountable for his sin—Adam was.

First, 1 Corinthians 7 clearly points out that the problem is a lack of self-control (v. 5). The problem lies with the spouse, or sometimes spouses, who lack self-control. In the case of a husband who struggles with pornography, he is to blame because he doesn't exercise the self-control to keep his sexual desires confined to the marital relationship. Self-control is an aspect of the fruit of the Spirit that is fostered, developed, and grown as you walk step-by-step with Christ. It is not your wife's responsibility to give you self-control or to fill in the gap for you when you aren't exercising it.

Second, the argument above leaves out other key biblical premises. Husbands who buy into that false argument are fond of quoting the first half of verse four: "For the wife does not have authority over her own body, but the husband does." But they like to ignore the implications of the second half: "Likewise the husband does not have authority over his own body, but the wife does." Horny husbands bring to this passage the presumption that it only goes in the direction of getting sex, but that is not the only implication. If a wife has authority over her husband's body, she has the authority to reject his advances as well. The verses in 1 Corinthians 7:1–5 are not justification for on-demand sex. It is a caution against withholding sex for long seasons of abstinence, but it does not condemn or take away the freedom of wives (or husbands) to say no to sex at times.

The harmful conclusion also leaves out what the Bible says about the heart, motivation, and the intended nature of sex. Sex, as God intended it, is designed to be a unique expression of love between a husband and wife. The intensity of the pleasure that comes from the sexual experience and orgasm are intended to bond husband and wife together. In a properly functioning marriage, a significant amount of the pleasure derived from sex comes from satisfying your spouse sexually (although even that can be twisted into selfish pride). Like all good gifts from the Creator, we misuse and abuse the gift of sex. We see the pleasure that it brings us as its chief purpose, and we go into sexual encounters primarily concerned about getting rather than giving.

A husband who is truly seeking to love his wife and honor his God will approach his wife sexually in humble service to her desires, including her desire not to have sex on given days. He will put aside forms of manipulation, like pouting, getting angry, giving gifts for sexual favors, isolating emotionally, withholding deep emotional conversation and connection except during times of sexual encounter, etc. He will lovingly accept his wife's refusal and not take it as a personal affront. When he does feel hurt, rejected, or excessively burdened with sexual temptation, he will first talk to God about it, and when appropriate, talk with his spouse about it in a loving, nondemanding, non-manipulative way.

As you grow closer to Christ and become more like him, you will become a better husband and better lover. As you put off pornography, masturbation, and selfish sexual advances, and put on humility, self-control, and sacrificial love, your wife will likely (but not guaranteed) become more attracted to you. Your sex life in marriage will become more satisfying because it will be more properly aligned with God's intended design. Yes, your wife, including her body and sexuality, are a gift from the Lord. Don't desecrate the gift and insult the gift giver through misuse, manipulation, or abuse.

Proverbs 5:18–19 offers this delightful instruction: "Let your fountain be blessed, and rejoice in the wife of your youth, a lovely deer, a graceful doe. Let her breasts fill you at all times with delight; be intoxicated always in her love." These are glorious words, and I pray you are able to live them out. But they are also couched in the context of warnings against sexual sin. The verses immediately before and after warn about the life-altering and sometimes life-ending consequences of pursuing sexual gratification outside of the marriage relationship. If you want a truly satisfying sexual relationship with your wife, then you must strive to put off sexual sin. Don't wait for her to respond the way you want her to before you determine to battle porn, and *never* blame her for your sinful sexual desires.

Questions for Action, Discussion, and Reflection

1. How have you responded to your wife in the past when she has tried to speak into your struggle with pornography? Whether you have been a Nabal or a David, take some time now and pray to God, thanking him for your wife and her willingness to stand up to you. Then go to your wife, confess any past sins in your responses, and ask forgiveness. Thank her for caring enough to speak truth.

2. Do you have a plan in place to keep your wife informed and involved with your pursuit of purity? If so, after reading this chapter, do you think it needs any revisions or updates? If you don't have such a plan, ask a wise biblical counselor or spiritual mentor to help the two of you develop a good transformation plan.

Further Reading

Powlison, David. *Making All Things New: Restoring Joy to the Sexually Broken*. Wheaton: Crossway, 2017.

Tripp, Paul David. *Sex in a Broken World: How Christ Redeems What Sin Distorts*. Wheaton: Crossway, 2018.

9

Amputations and Alterations

If your right eye causes you to sin, tear it out and throw it away. For it is better that you lose one of your members than that your whole body be thrown into hell.

—Matthew 5:29

WHETHER CAIN USED his bare hands, a rock, a stick, or a club to kill Abel we don't know. But from that moment forward, we have been inventing and innovating weapons to the point that one man can kill another with a piece of metal weighing less than 13 grams from a distance of over a mile away. Or by turning some keys and pressing a few buttons, the leader of one nation can virtually wipe out the population of another. Starvation is one strategy for defeating an enemy that has withstood the test of time. In ancient warfare, an army could surround a walled city and simply wait for the population to die off or surrender in the face of starvation. Today we cut off supply lines by bombing roads, setting up checkpoints, or enforcing no-fly zones, but the principle is the same. Cut off resources and your enemy will give up or die. Our spiritual battle with pornography can utilize this age-old strategy as well.

Amputation is the third A of the AAA. Don't worry, I'm not going to advocate for the removal of any body parts! While Jesus does prescribe gouging out your eye if it makes you lust (Matthew 5:29), he is speaking figuratively. The Bible does not endorse self-mutilation, but it does encourage radical amputation. When Jesus tells you to cut off your hand if it makes you sin, he is calling you to take desperate measures because you are in a desperate battle with sin. Amputation involves cutting off opportunities for temptation. The reality is that sin resides in us, so even if we took Jesus's command literally, we couldn't actually remove lust by tearing our eyes out, because lust resides in the heart (Matthew 15:19; Mark 7:21; James 1:14). However, our inward desires are often enticed and inflamed by temptations from without. The most important part of over-coming your sinful use of pornography is to direct your heart's thoughts, affections, desires, and choices toward Christ. But we also recognize the value of removing temptations that distract us from wholehearted worship and devotion to our Savior.

Romans 13:14 says, "But put on the Lord Jesus Christ, and make no provision for the flesh, to gratify its desires." In this one verse, we see the dynamic duo of admiration and amputation working together against sexual sin. The preceding verse offers the instruction to "walk properly as in the daytime, not in orgies and drunkenness, not in sexual immorality and sensuality, not in quarreling and jealousy" (Romans 13:13). If you are a believer in Jesus Christ, you have died to sin and been raised as a new creation (Romans 6:6; 2 Corinthians 5:17; Galatians 2:20; 5:24). You have been raised to a new life of walking with Christ that is enabled by Christ and is to be lived for Christ. But the spirit and the flesh still wage war with one another (Galatians 5:17).

Amputation without admiration and accountability is merely behavior change through circumstance modification. It will not last. The heart inclined toward sin will find an outlet of some kind. Even if you never watched another porn video or saw another illicit image, your mind has already been filled with images that may intrude or be recalled at any moment. Even without the data-base of images, the human heart is creative and can invent all kinds of fantasies without the external prompt of pornography. Yes, amputation will help, but it alone is not enough to transform you. True change comes when your heart is turned away from sin in repentance and toward Jesus in submission in order to be daily transformed by him. Keep that in mind as we discuss some of the benefits and practical applications of radical amputation.

Amputations

Whenever I think of amputation, I remember scenes from Civil War era movies with field hospitals that were nothing more than tents, often without sides to them. Under the tent, surgeons went from patient to patient with crude saws and knives to cut off the limbs of soldiers that had been mangled in combat. It is not a pretty scene. Thankfully, modern-day surgeries are much more sanitary, but they are still gruesome. There is nothing pretty about cutting off a body part. Doctors only amputate in extreme circumstances, when life hangs in the balance. The body part that is about to be severed poses a significant threat to the life of the one it is attached to. The limb must go, or life will be lost. Desperate times call for desperate measures. The reality is that if porn is a problem for you, there are things in your life that are a deadly threat to your soul. The Bible is clear that sin, left unchecked, festers and grows (Romans 1:21–32; 1 Corinthians 5:6; James 1:14–15). Sexual sin is especially invasive and pervasive. It threatens your marriage, your family, your livelihood, and your very soul (Proverbs 5:9–10; 6:26; 29:3). Wherever the sources of this temptation may be found, they must be removed.

The first step to radical amputation is identifying the sources and channels of temptation. You must be honest with yourself, your spouse, your counselor, your allies, and most of all with God about the sources of temptation in your life. For most today, pornography is usually accessed via the internet. The digital age we find ourselves in is fascinating and terrifying. We can find all kinds of information with a few touches on a screen or a simple voice command. This also means billions of sexually explicit images and videos are just as close. Right now, you probably have in your pocket or on your desk a phone that can access so much porn that you could never consume it all in a lifetime. In addition to your phone, every internet-enabled device in your life poses a threat.

Thankfully, there are many great digital allies to fight alongside you. I'll just say it plainly: if you struggle with porn, you must have some kind of accountability/filtering software on all your internet-enabled devices, period. There are many to choose from, and each has its own strengths and weaknesses. You and your transformation team will need to research the one that is right for you. You need to determine if you want filtering (those that block explicit content), monitoring options (tracks content and reports questionable material to accountability partners), or both. You need to find something that works with your operating system (iOS, Mac, PC, Android, etc.). Does it work on mobile devices or only computers? You will need something on all internet-enabled devices (desktop computers, laptops, tablets, gaming devices, phones, smart watches, etc.). It must work with your device and actually catch or block the avenues you use to access porn online. For example, some software only tracks the websites you visit on your phone's browser, but it can't track what you are doing via other apps on your phone. If those other apps access the internet or access illicit content in themselves (which includes basically all of your social media apps), then that blocking software is not sufficient.

One common question is whether to use free software or pay for software. I recommend going with a paid service. The primary reason people give for using free software is not being able to afford the paid option. My argument is simply, "You can't afford not to!" The costs incurred in your life by continuing to use porn, including but not limited to financial, far outweigh the small fee associated with paid accountability software. The paid options out there are very affordable and your purity is worth far more than a few cents a day. My primary concern with free services is that they are usually not updated often enough. Technology is constantly advancing, and ministries or companies that put out free software often cannot keep up with those advancements. Keep in mind that regardless of which software(s) you choose, amputation will fail if it is the only way you are fighting against pornography. No matter how good a software program is, you cannot put your trust in it to keep you from sin. If you don't work with Christ to transform your heart, you will find ways to circumvent your accountability software or find new places to access porn.

Even though accountability software is not sufficient on its own, that does not mean it isn't worth implementing. It typically takes significant effort to circumvent the protections offered by these applications. Even for the very tech savvy person, these software programs can put distance between you and your temptation. Making this sin a little harder for you to give in to provides more time for you to reflect on what you're doing and repent of your sinful desires before they come to fruition in sinful actions. It can also be invaluable for preventing your lust from being inflamed by accidentally stumbling upon an illicit image.

The point is that you must guard your heart by doing your best to cut off access to porn on your internet-enabled devices. If you can't, then get rid of the device. I know that may sound harsh, but remember Jesus's counsel in Matthew 5:29–30: "If your right eye causes you to sin, tear it out and throw it away. For it is better that you lose one of your members than that your whole body be thrown into hell. And if your right hand causes you to sin, cut it off and throw it away. For it is better that you lose one of your members than that your whole body go into hell."

While digital temptation is the most prevalent today, the internet is not the only source of illicit sexual temptation. There are still pornographic magazines, catalogs filled with scantily clad women, billboards, strip clubs, sexually explicit movies and music, prostitutes, women at the gym, etc., etc. You need to know your sources of temptation, share them with your transformation team (Jesus, your spouse, counselor, and allies), and make a plan to cut them out of your life. Some men have changed jobs because of temptation from flirtatious coworkers. Those are men who take Jesus's warning seriously, and they should inspire you to do the same. It is important to clarify that the temptation from without does not make you sin. The sinful desire lurks within your heart. You can't blame the woman at the gym for your lust. Even if you were completely isolated, living in an igloo in Antarctica, you could still lust. It is also important to remember that it would be impossible to remove every source of temptation from your life. The point is to identify the primary sources of temptation in your life and cut them off, no matter what it takes.

Failure to cut off sources of temptation may result in your eternal damnation. I am not teaching that you can lose your salvation, but rather a heart that is unwilling to take radical steps to overcome sin is a heart that does not belong to Jesus in the first place. If you find yourself being resistant to the majority of the advice in this book and the input of other mature believers, then you should take a hard look at your heart and consider whether or not you have truly repented of your sins and turned to Christ for salvation—or whether you still view yourself as the lord of your life (2 Corinthians 13:5-6). If you are having difficulty discerning this or feel fearful that you aren't really saved, talk about this with at least one other person on your transformation team. My desire and God's desire is not for you to constantly feel uncertain about the state of your soul, nor for you to feel a false sense of security because you go to church or you once prayed the "Sinner's Prayer." Even if you are certain that you have surrendered your life to Christ, take some time to examine how your heart is responding to the suggestions you have received from this book and your transformation team. Because of the fallen flesh that is still at work within us, our hearts are inclined to serve our own kingdoms rather than say to the Father, "Your kingdom come, your will be done, on earth as it is in heaven" (Matthew 6:10).

Take a moment now, and each day, to humble yourself before God and repent of any pride and hardness of heart that has made you unwilling to fight sin in the ways that you should.

Behind the Wire

Military members who are deployed to active theaters of operation (aka active war zones) know what it is like to live on high alert all the time. It is exhausting. It wears you out and grinds you down. They need a time and place where they can relax and let their guard down (or at least mostly down). They need to be able to get behind the wire, a phrase that describes a secure military installation. When they are out on patrol, they have to be constantly vigilant, which wears on a person physically, emotionally, mentally, and spiritually. Getting behind the wire allows them to rest and recuperate. They are only able to rest when they know that they are relatively safe from attacks.

My wife and I have sought to make our home a haven, a temptation-free zone. Your home should be the same for you. You need to work with your wife to set up safeguards so that your home is a place you can relax and let your guard down some. I recommend having router-based filtering software on your home network in addition to accountability software on your devices. This protects your whole home network so that guests can't intentionally or inadvertently bring porn into your home via the internet feed in your house (of course they can still access it via their cell phone data, so don't assume your child's friend can't access it just because they are in your house. Router-based security only affects your WIFI network). Also, purge your home of old movies that are sources of temptation. Fend off the Victoria's Secret catalogs and the like as though they were enemy combatants trying to overrun your home. Shut off cable, password protect your streaming services so that only your spouse can access them for you, build a wall so that you can't see your neighbor sunbathing

Amputations and Alterations

next door! Whatever you need to do to make your home a safe zone, do it. Get behind the wire!

I know you are probably thinking of all the reasons and excuses for not implementing these changes. As I discussed in the previous section, however, it is important to ask yourself why you are considering excuses. In some cases, you may be resistant because it just seems like more work than it's worth. I get it. It is hard. Those changes are not easy—that is why it's called *radical amputation*! Amputation hurts, but it is worth it. It can save your marriage and your life. I alluded earlier to the fact that your attitude towards radical amputation reveals a great deal about your heart. I don't expect you to jump up and down with excitement about these changes; it's okay to recognize they are hard. But if you aren't willing to do them, there are serious problems in your heart that you need to address with God.

Recent revelations about the deceased and disgraced apologist Ravi Zacharias should serve as a warning to you. When confronted with his sin and encouraged to get help and accountability, he refused. He denied that he had a problem and wouldn't let anyone look into his life at all. He had multiple phones and internet devices and wouldn't allow anyone to access them. Now we discover that he was hiding a long history of serious sexual misconduct. I don't know for sure about his eternal fate, but Jesus's words that we read before do not bode well for that man.

On the encouraging side, I want to hold out some carrots for you as well. There is an amazing sense of relief for your soul when you amputate sources of temptation, come clean about your sin, get accountability, and grow with Christ. Just like a soldier can rest when he is behind the wire, you will be able to rest easier when you don't have the tug of temptation in your pocket, when you aren't looking over your shoulder wondering when someone is going to find you out. From time to time, the tug of temptation comes, and I begrudge my internet securities. Those are good times of warning, reminding me that I am still a work in progress and need to draw closer to Christ. But more often than not, I am so thankful for the parameters we have put in place to cut off avenues of temptation. I don't have anxiety over the tug of temptation when I grab my phone or start surfing the web. I also have great joy and can celebrate with God the growth that he has worked and continues to work in my life.

Alterations

Besides cutting off opportunities for temptation, you can make other changes in your life that will help you grow in godliness. There are plenty more, but I want to offer a few to get you started: be exhilarated with your wife in sexual union, help your wife see her body as God does, serve others, and grow your gratitude.

Be Exhilarated with Your Wife

Let's look at Proverbs 5:18–19 again, "Let your fountain be blessed, and rejoice in the wife of your youth, a lovely deer, a graceful doe. Let her breasts fill you at all times with delight; be intoxicated always in her love." This is some pretty racy language set in the midst of some other racy language warning men about the dangers of adultery and illicit sexual temptations. Earlier in this book, I warned against the false interpretation of Scripture that leads men to believe they are entitled to on-demand sex in marriage. In that context, I want to remind you that your wife is not merely a tool, nor the primary tool, for you to overcome sexual sin. However, sex with your wife is a great gift from God. It can and should be enjoyed. When you are fascinated, exhilarated, and intoxicated with her love, you will be less inclined to pursue sexual gratification elsewhere. Sex between husband and wife that is done with great love and attention to one another's desires is mutually beneficial, mutually enjoyable, and glorifying to God.

So when you and your wife have reconciled to the point of reengaging in sex, move into it with renewed love and enjoyment.

Thank God for your wife and thank him for the sexual union you can have. As your relationship is rebuilt on trust, honesty, and open communication, your sexual relationship will deepen as well.

You might be wondering, *What if I'm not attracted to my wife? What then?* Before I give any answers, I need to ask some questions. When you say you aren't attracted to your wife, what do you mean? Do you mean you aren't attracted to her physically? Or you aren't attracted to her at all? If you say you aren't attracted to your wife at all, not even her character, personality, sense of humor, enjoyment of common interests, etc., then there are likely some underlying conflicts and issues that need to be addressed between the two of you in marriage counseling. I'd encourage you to pursue additional marriage counseling in conjunction with this book and the work you are doing to battle pornography in your life. There is always hope for growth and change; I know for certain that it is possible for you and your wife to draw closer to one another as you draw closer to God individually and mutually.

If you find yourself unattracted to your wife physically but attracted to her in other ways, I still have some further questions as to why you don't find your wife physically attractive. These questions are very sensitive and can easily be taken the wrong way, so please approach them cautiously, give me the benefit of the doubt, and don't discuss them with your wife—at least not before doing so with a wise biblical counselor.

The first few questions are intended to get at the larger question of how your view of what is beautiful has been shaped by pornography. Are there other women at your wife's age and stage of life that you find attractive? If not, then you have bought the lie that the beauty/porn industry has been selling, the lie that perpetual youth is the soul of true beauty. Like all good lies, there are kernels of truth at the center. The Bible recognizes that physical beauty and youth tend to go hand in hand (Esther 2:3, 7; Proverbs 5:18). However, where the porn industry and our culture in general goes awry is the claim that youthful beauty can and should be maintained throughout all of life. That is why the message of the overwhelmingly successful cosmetic/beauty industry is "If you want to look good, look young." Color your gray hair, get rid of wrinkles, tighten things that have gotten loose, lift things that have begun to sag, fight the signs of aging. The fact is that you can't stay young forever, nor should you want to. The Bible is clear that outer/physical beauty fades over time, but what is truly valuable and worthwhile grows and improves with age (Proverbs 31:30; 2 Corinthians 4:16). If you have bought into this lie because of the porn you have been watching, then you need to pray and ask God to renew your mind in a few ways. First, ask him to change your heart so that you see the world the way he does (1 Samuel 16:7). Ask that you look for true beauty that grows with time instead of fading away (2 Corinthians 4:16). Ask that he help you see the inner beauty of people, which is far more important and lasting than outer beauty (1 Timothy 2:9; 1 Peter 3:3–4). There is great hope for true change here. As you set aside pornography, you will naturally (by God's creative design) begin to see the world more truthfully as it really is. And as you pursue God and his plan for your life, you can be divinely transformed to think, feel, desire, and act as he does.

If you are a man who answered yes when asked whether or not you find other women attractive who are at the same age and stage of life as your wife, that doesn't mean you are off the hook. The problem still resides with you, not your wife. While you may not have fully bought the lie of perpetual youth, your heart still needs to change. You need to pray and ask God for the same things listed above and add to it prayers that the Lord would instill in your heart strong attraction for your wife. As one of my pastors once said, "Your wife needs to become the very definition of physical beauty for you. When there is a new wrinkle or a new bulge, that wrinkle or bulge adds to your understanding of physical beauty." But don't rely on mere physical attraction; begin the regular habit of meditating on the things you love about your wife. Write them down. Thank God for them. Speak them to her. Tell her that you love her. Write notes encouraging her and affirming her in what she does well, what you appreciate, and ways that you see God working in her life. Spend time with her. Talk with her. Go on dates with her. As you do these things in tandem with your pursuit of God, your attraction for your wife will grow. It is important to remember that porn has tempted you to believe that the beauty of others is there for your benefit and enjoyment. This can even distort the way you think of your wife's beauty. She is beautiful because God made her. He made her the way she is primarily for his glory, not your ogling. The fact that you get to enjoy her beauty is a side blessing, but not the central purpose. You need to shift your focus away from self-gratification to self-sacrificing love.

Help Your Wife See Her Body as God Does

While the previous section suggested you consider your perceptions of beauty and the potential impact pornography has had on those perceptions, another victim of porn use may be your wife's perception of her own beauty. It is common for women whose husbands struggle with pornography to wrestle with false thoughts and feelings about their bodies. Jenny's book has a section on this for wives, so if you are reading these together, I'd encourage you to talk to your wife and listen to how your porn use has negatively impacted her view of her own body. It may be advisable to have this conversation with a biblical counselor present, especially if you are still struggling with communication in your marriage.

Temptations to poor thinking in this area tend to move in one of two overarching directions (with lots of variations within these polar opposites). On one side, your wife may be tempted to discontentment with her body in a way that drives her to unhealthy or unhelpful pursuits of beauty. On the other side, she may be tempted just to throw in the towel altogether and give up on her body and physical appearance. Neither one of these extremes is good or right. This is a very sensitive topic so I want to warn you to move forward with caution. Depending on your wife's state, you may not be the person who needs to talk to her about her body image, but that doesn't mean you have no responsibility here. Let me suggest a few things to think about and do in regard to your wife's body and her perception of it.

First, you both need to be sure you have the right priorities and goals in mind when it comes to each of your bodies. As I mentioned above, the goal in all of life is to glorify and honor God. This overarching goal touches every part of life, including what we eat and drink (1 Corinthians 10:31). Earlier in the same book we are told that our sex life is another way we glorify God (1 Corinthians 6:20). So the way you care for your body matters to God. Our bodies are gifts from him, temples for his Holy Spirit (1 Corinthians 6:19) that we are entrusted with to steward for his purposes. Besides avoiding sinful uses of our bodies, the primary measurement for stewarding our bodies is health, not beauty. Both you and your wife need to keep this at the front and center in your hearts and conversations on body image. The goal is not for either of you to have bodies that look a certain way; the goal is to be healthy.

If you have noticed your wife leaning toward one of these extremes, she should discuss it with her biblical counselor as well as a doctor. Some things to watch for are extreme dieting, excessive exercise, negative comments about her body, or a desire to pursue cosmetic surgery to "fix" troubled areas. At the other extreme, your wife may not exercise, may eat very unhealthily, and may put little to no effort into her dress or appearance. It is especially important to notice if there has been a significant shift in her behavior in any of these areas. Regardless of whether or not you have noticed a drift in either direction, you should definitely pay attention and take the next step—ask questions.

As I mentioned, this topic is very sensitive. One of the best ways to approach sensitive topics is with questions. You want to make them as nonjudgmental as possible, and if you are concerned that your motive will be misunderstood, simply clarify your motive when you ask. We are giving you an on-ramp to this conversation by including the topic in our books so that hopefully you will be able to approach it more naturally. Even if you are not reading together, you can ask your wife something like, "Honey, has my pornography use impacted the way you see yourself or your body?" Be sure to ask in a time and place where you won't be interrupted and you will have some time to talk. She may need time to think about it, so don't push. Let her know you are willing to give her time to think about it. You can also tell her you want to know so that you can understand the impact of your sin and use it as further fuel to fight temptation. Again, it may be better to have this conversation with a biblical counselor present, especially if difficult conversations are a source of contention and strife in your marriage.

When you ask these questions, your biggest jobs are to listen, learn, and pray for her. Let her know that you are grieved over how your sin has impacted her in all areas of life, including this one. Don't get defensive, and don't try to argue with her about it. Listen, learn, and love her. As you put off pornography and give your attention and love to her in godly ways, your actions will speak far louder than any affirming words. That is not to say you should never tell her she is beautiful (you should), but I am saying that your actions need to match those words so that she is better able to believe them.

Serve Others

Pornography is inherently selfish. As you put off porn, put on love for others, especially your wife. Take time that you would have used to view porn and write notes of encouragement. Ask your wife what you can do around the house to help her out. Take her on dates. Ask her how you can best express love to her.

Don't limit your selfless service to your wife. Instead, seek out opportunities to serve in all of your current relationships, and look for new people you can know and serve. Help your kids with their homework or sports practice, or take up a new hobby together. Reach out to your neighbors and see if there are ways you can serve them. Get involved in your local church in some service ministry. As you serve others, your tendency toward self-ishness will diminish.

Selfless love, sacrifice, and humility are key characteristics of our Savior, Jesus. Philippians 2 describes Christ's humble nature and encourages us to have the same attitude in ourselves (verse 5). This attitude manifests itself by looking out for the interests of others before our own, thinking of others as more significant than ourselves, and not allowing selfish ambition or conceit to be our motivation (Philippians 2:3–4). As we grow and are transformed to be like him, we want to see these key character traits grow in us. This transformation happens from the inside out. As you put on these heart attitudes and motivations, it will also help correct the underlying sins and temptations that are driving you to porn use. If you have gone to porn to satisfy a longing for power, put-ting on Christlike humility will assuage your craving for power. If you have gone to porn to make you feel important or significant, finding your significance in Christ and what he says about you will meet that good desire.

Grow in Gratitude

Earlier I mentioned that one implication of your struggle with pornography is that you are discontent with the sexual relation-ship God has blessed you with in your marriage. I know some of you will push back against that idea. Some interpret that as saying you don't think your wife is attractive or that you don't enjoy having sex with her. For some people that is the case, but often it is not. Many men who struggle with porn greatly enjoy the sexual relationship that they have with their spouse, and many men who struggle with porn think their wives are beautiful. So they fight and say, "I am content with my wife. I am content with our sex life." But discontentment does not mean disfavor. Discontentment means not being satisfied with the good things that we have been given. If you were truly and fully satisfied with all that God has given you, then you would not be pursuing sinful alternatives that he has not provided. If you were content with your wife and your sexual relationship, you wouldn't pursue porn. One of the Bible's most powerful tools against discontentment is thankfulness. Therefore, one of the tools in your arsenal to help you fight against pornography is growing in gratitude.

The Bible teaches us that we should "give thanks in all circumstances" (1 Thessalonians 5:18). This may seem impossible, especially when you are going through the challenges you are right now in your battle with pornography. However, it is possible. First and foremost, you can and should always give thanks to God for who he is and what he does. You can always praise him and thank him for the sacrificial love that he has poured out on you, most acutely in the crucifixion of Jesus. You can always thank him for the new and eternal life won for you in the resurrection.

In addition to the theological truths I mentioned above, I encourage you to begin keeping a list of things that you are thankful for. Philippians 4:4–9 has some great counsel for trying times, and one aspect of that counsel is to let your minds dwell on "whatever is true, whatever is honorable, whatever is just, whatever is pure, whatever is lovely, whatever is commendable, if there is any excellence, if there is anything worthy of praise" (Philippians 4:8). This includes grand theological truths, Scripture, and things you learn in sermons, but it also includes little things like the smell of a flower, the taste of chocolate, and the comfort of your favorite chair. You can grow in gratitude by practicing it. Take a piece of paper or open the notes app in your phone and start writing a list of things you are thankful for. When you are finished, pray to God and thank him for those things. Next time you are tempted to look up porn or dwell on some illicit sexual image, pull out that list and start thanking God. Take some time to add a couple of things to the list while you are at it.

Put Your Plan to Paper

"Failing to prepare is preparing to fail." "Prior, proper, planning prevents poor performance." These axioms have flowed through my ears in a variety of contexts athletics, military, productivity reading, and many more. They are prevalent because they are powerfully true. Now that we have discussed many of the important elements of change that you can implement in your life, it is time to create a transformation plan that is tailored for you and put that plan to paper. You will want to work with your transformation team (God, your wife, your biblical counselor, local and long-term allies, etc.) to devise this plan. Once you draft it, send it to each of them and ask for feedback. Edit the plan until everyone on your team is satisfied, and then share the final transformation plan with everyone.

Start by writing down the common areas of temptation for yourself. Then come up with a solution to remove, thwart, or block those temptations. This includes your accountability software, router-based filtering, cancellation of magazines or catalogs, alternate driving routes to avoid alluring storefronts, etc. Write these measures down.

Next, determine a regular schedule for accountability conversations. How often will you check in with your local allies? What about your long-term ally? How often will you report to your wife on this struggle? Write it down on the plan, then schedule those meetings on your calendar (make sure your allies do too). Are there specific questions you want them to ask you periodically? If so, write them down and tell your accountability partners how often to ask (i.e. weekly calls, but ask these questions every other week).

What is your plan to handle the unexpected temptations? Will you call or text one of your allies to let them know of the temptation? What about times when you are tempted to circumvent your safeguards? Have a plan to call in reinforcements. Maybe you can devise a code phrase for your allies that you text them to let them know to pray for you and call you.

What will you do if you give into temptation? Who will you tell? When will you tell them? Will there be any steps taken to prevent future lapses?

Which Bible verses can you memorize and meditate on that will help you fight temptation and put your mind on Christ? List them, and come up with a plan to begin memorizing them.

What is your plan for habits of holiness? How often will you read your Bible, pray, meditate, fast, etc.? Get specific, and write it down. For example, "I will read my Bible daily for twenty minutes at 6:30 a.m., pray for ten minutes, and then spend five minutes working on Scripture memory. I'm going to start by reading one chapter a day from the book of John."

Include in your plan the alterations you hope to add into your life as well. How will you begin serving others? What will you do to grow in gratitude?

After you have revised this document to the satisfaction of your allies and yourself, give them a copy. Make a schedule to review it periodically, as well and revise it as needed. Remember, however, that the transformation plan is not Scripture, it is not written in stone, and it should not become a legalistic burden. It is a tool to help you in the process of becoming more like Jesus. It is meant to help you put off sin and put on righteousness.

Fight Back!

The AAA of fighting sin is admiration, accountability, and amputation. This chapter has shown you the importance of cutting off sources of temptation in your life, and it has guided you toward some things you can put on (or further develop) that will help you grow. We noted earlier that amputation and accountability without admiration is mere behavior modification. Don't put all your hope in accountability software or conversations with godly men because, by themselves, they will fail. But don't allow past failure in these areas to cause you to disregard the good that can come through them. Porn is an enemy that is seeking to destroy you. Fight back by choking out the sources of temptation that feed your desire for it.

Questions for Action, Discussion, and Reflection

1. Recruit two to three people to be allies with you in this fight against pornography.

2. Write the first draft of your pornography transformation plan, and share it with your allies.

3. Create a list of things you are thankful for. Start with at least five. Keep it with you. Each time you are tempted to look at porn, pull out that list, thank God for three to five of the things on the list, and add one more.

Further Reading

Owen, John. *The Mortification of Sin.* Carlisle, PA: Banner of Truth, 2004.

10
Living Like David

IF YOU ARE like me and millions (perhaps billions) of other people who have occupied this planet in the last fortyish years, you have some affinity for, or at least knowledge of, the Star Wars movie franchise. Like all good stories, the Star Wars films have their share of heroes and villains. And, like most modern movies, the heroes do not always behave heroically. Han Solo is one such character. If you were to isolate specific scenes from the movies, Han would show himself to be a self-serving, smug, arrogant criminal who is only interested in self-preservation and accumulating wealth. But as the films unfold, we gain a different perspective on Han. When you step back and assess Han, you have to put him in the hero category even though, at times, he acts in villainous ways. The life of David, which is detailed in the pages of Scripture, is much the same. David's life is full of villainous deeds, but in the final assessment, he is remembered as the greatest king of Israel and a man after God's own heart.

As I discussed in the chapter on admiration, your transformation into being like Jesus will not be complete until Christ returns or you go to meet him. In this life we can never be exactly like Jesus, but we can grow in our similarity to him. Like many of the examples we have in Scripture, we can become a type of

Christ that displays his likeness for the entire world to see. King David is one of the strongest types of Christ in the Old Testament. The forefather of Jesus, he sat on the throne of Israel, ruling over God's chosen people. He willingly put his life on the line to rescue and save God's people. He is described as a man after God's own heart (1 Samuel 13:14; Acts 13:22). But David was no angel. We've already discussed some of those less-than-Christlike scenes from David's life. David, as he is depicted in the Bible, is not a man who demonstrates faithfulness every moment of his life. Yes, he had some pretty amazing moments of faithfulness (killing lions and bears to protect his father's flock, killing Goliath, writing many of the Psalms, etc.), but his life is also speckled with moments of huge, catastrophic failure. I mean, come on, the guy committed rape and murder! But God still says that David's heart reflected his own. How is that possible? One of my mentors put it this way: "Your life is not a snapshot or a collection of photos, it is a film-strip." Back before digital photography, movies were actually pro-jected onto screens by shining light through a running filmstrip. A movie was a series of pictures all strung together and played at high speed, one after another. If you look at one frame, you don't get the whole story. Our lives are similar; we are not defined by our worst moments or our best moments. As with Han Solo and David, we have to step back and take in the whole story. If you, or I, or your spouse only look at you through the lens of your porn use, we will see a twisted, distorted view of your life.

More important than specific moments is the direction and trajectory of your life. Are you moving toward God or away from him? Taken the wrong way, this could sound like the false view that many people hold—the idea that God weighs our good and our bad deeds, and as long as the scale tips toward the good, we are in. Please hear me: that is not what I'm saying.

To make another film analogy, God is not a moviegoer who watches and then determines at the end whether the characters are heroes or villains. He is the screenwriter, producer, director, and star. We are the cast, the supporting actors, and the actresses. We are there to highlight the central star, who is Jesus. Our lives are intended to make Jesus look good, and in the end, whether we cooperate or not, that is exactly what we do. The star of the show always ends up being the star. All the other characters, good guys and bad, despite their best or worst intentions, add to the star's shine. The question is whether you want to be a supporting actor who joins forces with the star to make him shine, or a villain who works against him but still ends up making him look good while you look like a fool. Those characters that come alongside the star hero are influenced by him and begin to take on his characteristics. They become more heroic the longer they are with this hero. Han Solo became more hero than villain the longer he hung out with Luke Skywalker. A heart redeemed by God will be gradually transformed to look like Jesus. As we described before, it is an up and down journey. In certain scenes of our lives, those watching might be wondering if we are really villains, and yet, at other times we will look like heroes. But in the end, the final assessment is not based on the balance of our good deeds versus our bad deeds, but on how closely we walked with and were transformed by the star of all life, Jesus.

I'm not going to sugarcoat it for you—walking in faithful repentance is hard. It takes sweat and perseverance. There will be seasons of faltering, seasons of doubt, and seasons of discouragement. There will be times when you hurt others and when they hurt you. Through it all, Jesus will be there as an example, a source of motivation and inspiration, your friend and ally, and, most of all, your loving Savior.

You walked into a pawnshop with more than your wife's wedding ring to peddle. You sold away her heart and your own. No matter how hard you try, no matter how much you work, you can never pay the price required to buy them back, to erase what you have done. But praise be to God for Jesus Christ our Lord who has gone into that store and paid the shop owner with a payment far more valuable than gold or silver. He paid your debt with his own blood and redeemed you. He has redeemed you for your good and his glory. He is also the one who can redeem your marriage.

Questions for Reflection:

1. What now? Where do you go from here? If you haven't started implementing the counsel laid out in this book—start. Start by talking to someone, then get them to help you in this journey.

2. Who will your transformation team consist of in addition to Jesus and your wife?

Further Reading

Ortlund, Ray. *The Death of Porn: Men of Integrity Building a World of Nobility.* Wheaton: Crossway, 2021.

Appendix 1
Porn and Abuse[1]

Dear Reader,

THANK YOU FOR investing the time it took to read this book. I pray the investment is one that will have great return in your life in the form of growing godliness. It may seem odd to have a section on abuse in a book devoted to helping people overcome their struggle with pornography. The best explanation I can give is to reference a recent conversation with my friend Chris Moles, who said, "Pornography and abuse are two symptoms of the same heart." The sad reality is pornography use and abuse are common companions. The purpose of this appendix is to serve as a mirror for self-reflection and evaluation. I pray this book has helped you grow in humility and the ability to identify sin in your life. I also pray that you will read this appendix with increasing humility to examine your life and see if the heart that has lead you to use pornography has also acted out in abusive ways to your spouse. Again, this exercise will be most beneficial if it is done in relationship with a biblical counselor who knows you, loves you, and can help you discern what is taking place in your heart and life.

The heart behind both abuse and pornography use is a heart that has self at the center. It is a heart that is bent, first and foremost, on getting what it wants. It is the heart that places its desire above everything to the point that other people are primarily a means to getting what it desires. Pornography objectifies women. You've probably heard this before, but what do you think it means? It means people viewing pornography aren't looking at women as women. They don't see the people in the images as human beings created in God's image to glorify and honor him. When we look at porn, we aren't thinking about that woman's relationships, her beliefs, her purpose, or her interests. Pornography users are focused on themselves and their desires. The people in the depictions they watch are objects, things, and implements to be used to gratify their sexual cravings.

Abusers also view people as objects, as means to an end, not ends in and of themselves. People are not seen as creations of God to love, humbly defer to, and to serve, but as servants to their desires. Again, self is at the center of the heart. Everything and everyone exist for the purpose of fulfilling their desires. Abuse moves a step further when it deploys force of some kind to overcoming obstacles to fulfilling a desire. Abuse involves coercion, the utilization of power to subordinate, manipulate, and control someone. People become servants of your will, not the will of God. The force employed can be physical. Most people think of physical violence when they hear abuse, but it is not only physical violence that is abuse. Using financial power, relational dynamics, emotional manipulation, cognitive coercion, words, or anything else that one can employ to subjugate and control another person is abuse of some kind.

I don't know if you have engaged in abusive behavior, but I can tell you that the heart that led you to look at porn is the same heart that may lead you down that road if you haven't traveled it already. If you are not an abuser, I pray you take this as a warning to turn your heart toward Christ. Turn to be a man who loves and serves others as you follow the example of our Savior. If you know that you have abused your spouse, please seek help from a wise, trained biblical counselor who can help you overcome this sin, as well as your pornography use. Abuse is a far more serious concern and should take priority over your counseling for pornography use. If you are not sure where you stand, the following section will help you examine your life for abusive tendencies.

Warning Signs of Abuse

Here are some behaviors that often take place in an abusive relationship. As you read these questions, preferably with a trustworthy friend, consider whether or not they occur in your relationship.[2] As you read these, ask yourself, "Do I do the following to my spouse or in our relationship?"

❏ Embarrass or humiliate her in front of others?
❏ Push, grab or shove her?
❏ Lie to her regularly?
❏ Make her feel like she is walking on eggshells?
❏ Often seem angry at someone or something?
❏ Deprive her of sleep?
❏ Tell her how to dress or act?
❏ Pressure her for sex in ways that make her feel uncomfortable?
❏ Make her feel crazy?
❏ Use weapons to scare her?
❏ Ignore her or give her the silent treatment?
❏ Blame her for how you treat her, or for anything bad that happens?
❏ Check up on her excessively?
❏ Use the children to control her? Try to turn the children against her?
❏ Make all the decisions about money without her?
❏ Try to isolate her by controlling where she goes, who she sees, and what she does?
❏ Intimidate her with looks, gestures, cursing, or a loud voice?

☐ Degrade her, make her feel insignificant, powerless and/or worthless?

☐ Slap, pinch, push, or kick her?

☐ Choke her?

☐ Minimize or deny your abusive behavior?

☐ Threaten to hurt or punish her if she doesn't do what you want?

☐ Threaten to leave her, hurt her, or commit suicide?

☐ Act extremely jealous?

☐ Often criticize her, her friends, or her family?

☐ Destroy her property, possessions, or documents?

In addition to the questions above, I want to encourage you to look specifically at your porn use to see if it is also abusive. Not because abuse and porn always go hand in hand, but they can, and a porn user who continues unabated will often turn into an abuser of some kind. The line between porn use of an abuser and that of a non-abuser is vague and I won't try to make a clear line where one doesn't exist. Porn use is evil and needs to be put aside no matter what, but abusive porn use may require more intervention.

Porn use in an abusive marriage may not lead to acts of sexual violence against a wife (though it often will). That is not what defines it as abusive. An abuser may use pornography in the same ways as many other men but his heart overflows with entitlement, objectification, intention to shame, and control. He will manipulate and use sex/pornography to get what he wants.

Control is a central element of abuse. An abuser will crave porn for the power he feels from it not simply the gratification of voyeuristic desires. The control and power he craves will often be manifesting in the types of porn he watches, how he uses it, and in other non-sexual areas of life as well.

Often an abusive husband who uses pornography will exhibit some of the following behaviors:

1. He demands sex.
2. He threatens using porn if he doesn't get what he wants from her. "If you don't have sex with me I'm going to look at porn," or, "If you don't do _____ I'll watch porn." He may threaten extramarital relations, "If you don't do _____ I'll find someone else who will."
3. He may abandon sex with his wife, only getting sexual gratification from pornography.
4. He forces his wife to do sexual acts that she is uncomfortable with.
5. Sex is primarily about satisfying him, his desires, not pleasing his wife. It is another form of objectifying his wife and not treating her as a person, equally valuable and made in the image of God.
6. He uses pornography as a menu of sexual acts he would like his wife to perform.
7. He punishes her for not complying with his sexual desires.
8. He may force/coerce her to watch pornography.
9. He may force her to make "homemade porn." If she complies he will also often use those pornographic images against her. For example, he may threaten, "If you tell anyone I'll show this to your parents (boss, friends, pastor, kids, etc.)."
10. He may watch violent porn. This will often lead to acts of violence in the sexual relationship.
11. He derives pleasure from seeing his wife denigrated, hurt, or fearful during sex.
12. He may force his wife to allow or invite other people to participate in their sexual relationship.

If any of these behaviors are present, please reach out to your biblical counselor right now and talk to him about what has been going on. You can also find resources to help or sign up for Men of Peace groups at chrismoles.org.

Resources for more information on abuse and how to deal with it:

Books:

Moles, Chris. *The Heart of Domestic Abuse: Gospel Solutions for Men Who Use Control and Violence in the Home*. Minneapolis: Focus Publishing, 2015.

Strickland, Darby. *Is it Abuse: A Biblical Guide to Identifying Domestic Abuse and Helping Victims*. Phillipsburg, NJ: P&R Publishing, 2020.

Online:

darbystrickland.com
chrismoles.com

The following have multiple resources on abuse that you can access by searching "abuse":

Biblical Counseling Coalition, biblicalcc.org
Christian Counseling and Educational Foundation, ccef.org
Association of Biblical Counselors, christiancounseling.com
Association of Certified Biblical Counselors, biblicalcounseling.com

Appendix 2
Ministry after Porn

EVEN IF YOU don't have a "ministry job," I want to encourage you to read this appendix—both for your own soul and for others that you might have a chance to minister to. Even if you don't work in "vocational ministry," many of the lies that Satan uses to take pastors out of the pulpit can be turned on you, to keep you from doing the good works that God has called you to do. You may have stepped out of volunteer ministry because your struggle with porn left you thinking that God would never use someone who struggles with sexual sin to serve in his church. The pages that follow will encourage you to reengage in the ministry God has called you to. God may also put you in the path of a pastor, missionary, or someone else serving in vocational ministry that struggles with porn. You can then use the comfort God has given you in your struggle to help them in theirs (2 Corinthians 1:3–4). So please keep reading.

My wife and I have been married for more than 18 years and have navigated many phases of ministry life. Together we've attended seminary and served the church both on a voluntary basis and through full-time vocational ministry (pastoring in the local church and directing parachurch organizations). When we first started out, good advice for individuals struggling with pornography was sparse—and especially sparse for women whose husbands were struggling with pornography. There were occasions that we needed help but didn't know where to turn for guidance. So we want to provide this appendix to answer some of the very questions that we had ourselves and have since heard from others.

Question 1: Does any pornography use automatically disqualify me from leadership in Christian ministry?

If you have read this book, then you understand that we do not believe pornography use automatically disqualifies someone from leadership in Christian ministry. If you skipped ahead to this section without reading the book, now you know. Of course, giving the simple answer no to this question would not suffice. The question is more complex and requires further explanation.

Before we delve deeper into this question, we want to make it clear that we do not speak for every Christian, nor do we claim to have absolute authority on this matter. There are many godly men and women who will disagree with the position we take. You, the reader, must weigh our words (and the words of those who disagree) against the only infallible, fully authoritative source of knowledge we have—the Bible. We will do our best to explain our position and support it biblically. If you are on staff at a church or considering a ministry role at a church where the leadership/ church policies differ from the position articulated below, then you need to submit to that leadership/church policy. Feel free to use our material to try to persuade them otherwise, but do not create division in the church over this issue. Respect and submit to the authorities that God has placed over that local congregation, whether you agree with them or not. If you cannot do so in good conscience, then you should not accept a position in that church, and you should consider moving to another ministry if you must.

There are so many variables at play in each person's situation that it would be impossible for us to address every single one.

You need to have open and honest conversations about your particular situation with your spouse and the spiritual shepherds in your life. This is necessary whether you are in ministry already or considering future ministry options. You need to remove yourself as the primary decision maker in these conversations and be willing to submit to the wisdom of your pastor/elders (Hebrews 13:17). You need to be honest about the amount (frequency and duration of each incident, length of time this has been going on) and type (photos, videos, hetero, homo, child, or violent, etc.) of pornography you are consuming. You need to disclose the steps you have taken to battle this sin, the steps you have taken to undermine your battle, and the ways in which you have deceived those around you. This is important knowledge to help you and your church family battle your pornography use and decide whether or not you should be a ministry leader. Some types of pornography use are illegal and would necessitate the involvement of legal authorities. If the spiritual shepherds in your life do not feel equipped to assess your situation, they can consult a wise biblical counselor. Solomon SoulCare offers consulting services to counselors, pastors, and ministries. If the leadership surrounding you is unsure of how to proceed, they can visit solomonsoulcare.com to schedule a consultation. You can also visit the Biblical Counseling Coalition's website (biblical counselingcoalition.org) which has a "Find a Counselor" page that lists many biblical counselors and also links to other organizations that have counselor listings.

As mentioned above, we do not believe that pornography use automatically disqualifies someone from leadership in Christian ministry. What lies at the center of our concern is the state and inclination of your heart toward your sin and your Savior. The qualifications of elder/pastor in 1 Timothy 3 and Titus 1 must be consulted and used to evaluate you and your qualification for those specific roles, but other passages should be brought to bear to help you (and others around you) consider your heart. These verses include Matthew 3:8; 5:6; Luke 3:8; Acts 26:20; Romans 7; 2 Corinthians 7; Galatians 5; and Philippians 2.

With these passages in mind, you and the shepherds of your local church need to consider the following questions:

1. What is the general inclination of your heart? Are you generally moving toward Christ and desiring to be more like him?
2. Do you genuinely hate your sin and long to be rid of it (Romans 7)?
3. Do you brazenly pursue your lusts for pornography?
4. Is there genuine brokenness over your sin and a desire to forsake it and move toward Jesus (2 Corinthians 7)?
5. Looking at the totality of your life, which do you generally manifest—the deeds of the flesh or the fruit of the Spirit (Galatians 5)?
6. Do you hunger and thirst for righteousness (Matthew 5:6)?
7. Are you willing to humbly submit to the instruction, accountability measures, and oversight of your spiritual shepherds (Philippians 2; Hebrews 13)?
8. Are you actively seeking out ways to undermine, thwart, or skirt around the accountability measures in your life?
9. Is there evidence of genuine repentance in your life in both attitude and action (Matthew 3:8; Luke 3:8; 2 Corinthians 7)?
10. Are you willing to involve others in the accountability process with an open and welcoming heart?

These questions are designed to reveal deeper heart attitudes rather than mere behavioral responses. Some people will appear repentant for a season as they conform to the external constraints imposed upon them. However, if their hearts are not genuinely transformed, they will inevitably return to pornography. Left unchecked, it is likely they will move beyond pornography into deeper sexual sins. If there is pride, refusal to be fully open and honest, a lack of desire to repent, or resistance to outside accountability and help, then those who are in a shepherding role should be concerned and consider steps to remove this person from ministry. Those who are genuinely repentant will likely still struggle, but they will also experience growth toward Christlikeness. There should be evidence of brokenness over sin, commitment to forsake the sin, a humble desire for oversight and accountability, and active demonstrations of repentance and growth over time.

When you consider the qualifications of an elder from 1 Timothy 3 and Titus 1, the words *above reproach* and *blameless* stand out as glaring condemnations for those who struggle with pornography use. While a full exegesis of these passages is outside the scope of this book, I want to offer these words of encouragement from one commentator discussing these words in Titus 1:6, 7:

> The only two other New Testament passages that contain this word suggest another possibility for explaining what Paul has in mind. First, Paul assures the Corinthians that Jesus Christ 'will also keep you firm to the end, so that you will be blameless on the day of our Lord Jesus Christ' (1 Cor 1:8). Paul is not saying the Corinthians are presently perfect; his epistle to them is proof of the contrary. They are not even blameless in Paul's assessment, from a doctrinal and ethical point of view. He is rather speaking of them as believers 'in Christ.' As those who have believed and received the grace of the gospel (see 1 Cor 1:4–6), they possess a righteousness through faith that assures them of God's present, as well as eschatological, exoneration. They are blameless in God's sight by virtue of the sufficiency of Christ's death for their sake.[1]

When God calls pastors/elders to be "above reproach," it is not a requirement of perfection, nor is it something that people can create in themselves. It is only something that is accomplished in the completed work of Christ. If you are truly running to and relying on Christ to be transformed, then there is hope and assurance that you will grow (Philippians 1:6).

Question 2: If I have multiple relapses into pornography use, does that disqualify me from ministry?

This is a follow-up question to the first one. We would apply similar principles as in our answer above but encourage the church leaders/shepherds involved to examine your history more carefully. The primary concern is whether or not you are genuinely repentant and seeking to grow or whether your repeated struggle with porn is evidence that your heart is not inclined toward God but toward self and feeding this sin.

Some additional questions to ask in these situations:

1. How many times has this been an issue?
2. Tell us about each period of pornography use in the past. What led to each incident (context of what was going on in life, what preceded the initial return that time—accidentally stumbled across enticing images, actively pursued pornography, etc.)? How long did it last? What kinds of pornography were you viewing (see questions in the previous section)?
3. What led to your sin being exposed (was it voluntary disclosure or involuntary discovery)?
4. What did you do at that time to forsake your sin?
5. Were there attempts to undermine your accountability?
6. How did you grow or change between incidents?

This sixth question is a difficult question to wrestle through, and you, along with your church leaders, must ask God for wisdom in discerning your heart. The goal is to seek to understand your heart from God's perspective. Are you a believer who is genuinely struggling and growing, or someone who keeps returning to this sin because it is what you truly love and worship? There should be signs that you are growing. These signs are manifest through decreasing frequency, longer periods of abstaining from pornography, and growth toward Christ. However, we also must be careful not to create arbitrary timelines or measurements of repentance (i.e., "three strikes you're out").

It is important to note that pornography use can disqualify a person from pastoral ministry. For instance, a pattern of chronic pornography use would violate the qualifications of an elder in Titus 1:7–8. A person who wrestles in this way is not demonstrating self-control, is not disciplined, and is not above reproach.

Question 3: I am a seminary student, and I struggle with pornography. What should accountability look like in this phase of life? Should I even be pursuing ministry?

Accountability for each phase of life should include people who are close to you in proximity and those who are well acquainted with you and your struggle. Preferably there is overlap, but in seasons where you are transient (seminary) or new (landing in a new ministry), you are going to rely most on those who have known you for some time, even though they may be far off. However, you need to be proactive in your search for someone where you gather regularly for worship who will provide you accountability. If you have not had accountability in the past, then you need to start *now* wherever you are. When you are serving in a ministry or on staff with a ministry, it is essential that someone in leadership over you is made aware of the problem as soon as possible. This means that if you have not disclosed this already, you need to make a plan (preferably with your spouse and counselor) to meet with your pastor/supervisor/board of director member and share openly and honestly about your struggle.

This also means that when you are moving to a new position you need to be forthright about your struggle and pertinent sexual history. This will actually be an excellent way for you to clarify whether this is a good ministry for you to be a part of and establish a strong, transparent, trusting relationship early in your ministry. It will alleviate any fear or worry that your sin will be discovered. This will eliminate any doubt about whether or not you would have gotten the job if they really knew what you were like. It will kill the doubts that creep in, whispering that somehow your sin is the source of difficulty in ministry. All these thoughts will assail you in ministry as ammunition of the enemy to undermine what God wants to accomplish in and through you.

If you are currently a seminary student struggling with porn and you are wondering whether you should even pursue ministry, this can only be answered in the context of community. This is a question that your local church family can help you answer. They will only be able to apply wisdom to this question if you are fully transparent with them—they need to know who you really are and how you really struggle, in order to confirm your calling to ministry (or encourage you to take a break from seminary in order to pursue personal growth). You need to honestly disclose every aspect of your history with porn use/sexual sin with a few wise leaders in your church (the questions listed in Question 1 and 2 of this appendix and disclosure questions in Chapter 4 are good places to start). Then ask those leaders to help you discern whether or not seminary is the best place for you right now. If you are considering seminary, these transparent conversations will prepare you for conversations that will need to take place in future ministry interviews. If you are currently a seminary student, those hard conversations need to happen without delay.

Question 4: We are currently in the process of interviewing with churches for ministry positions. We wonder if, when, how, and to who should we disclose the struggle with pornography.

This is a tricky question because it doesn't have one clear answer for every situation. The answer will come through discernment, prayer, and seeking wise counsel. One thing that is absolutely clear is that before you accept a new ministry position, someone in leadership needs to know. In most cases we wouldn't recommend that someone put this on a resume or other documentation that is requested in the early phases of the hiring process. It is better disclosed face-to-face so that clarifying questions can be asked and opportunities for confusion are minimized. As you proceed through the process you will likely be interviewed via telephone or video chat, then have for one or two in-person interviews (this is especially true with churches). As the process progresses, you will begin to build relationships with the people involved in leadership in the church. This will help you gain comfort and wisdom about when to disclose your struggle and to whom. Pray specifically for wisdom regarding this matter and recruit others to pray for you (your wife, current accountability allies, etc.). Trust God to open up the opportunity—then take it. We can't give you a detailed time line, but we insist that you do it before you accept the position.

Question 5: As a pastor, should my accountability come from inside or outside the church that I am pastoring?

The answer is both. Ideally, every pastor should have men within the church and outside the church who know him intimately and can be sources of encouragement and accountability in all matters of life, including his struggle with sexual temptations. There are many pastors who avoid accountability within the church because they are afraid that their sin will be used against them or that people will lose respect for them as a shepherd. But when has our obedience ever been dependent upon whether or not others will behave appropriately? When is it ever good to make decisions based on fear? When has God ever called his under-shepherds to pretend to be something they are not or to act as though they have no sin? Where does Scripture say that there is a lesser expectation or demand for obedience from the leaders of the church than the other members? Quite the opposite, God's Word says that leaders will be held to a higher account (Luke 12:48; James 3:1). God tells us he has not given us a spirit of fear but of power (2 Timothy 1:7). God's Word tells us that if we say we have no sin or have not sinned, we are self-deceived, liars, we make God out to be a liar, and his word is not in us (1 John 1:8–10). God's Word calls us to faithfulness despite the accusations of others, both true and false.

We convince ourselves that if people know about our sin it will damage our ministry and the church. But which is more damaging—revealing the truth and demonstrating how God calls people to overcome sin or hiding it and pretending we are somehow above the sins that are common to every man? What is more damaging—shining light into the dark places or pretending they don't exist and allowing sin to fester and grow there until it is discovered? What is more damaging—a pastor who is humble and acknowledges his sin and dependence upon God and the work of Christ or the one who promotes a false vision of self-righteousness and independence? Which has been more damaging to the church—pastors who walked in humility or those whose pride lead them to public failure? Think about your own experience with other ministry leaders. What did it do to you when a pastor was willing to be open and honest about his sin struggles, his weakness, and his dependence upon Christ, his Spirit, the Word of God, and the church? On the other hand, what does it do to you each time you hear of another church leader who has fallen from his false pedestal, tearing down his ministry, tearing apart his family, and disgracing the name of Christ?

You are living proof of the statistics we cited before. The question is not whether or not pastors struggle with porn—they do, you do. The question is what are we going to do about it? Silence on the matter has not resolved the problem; instead, it has likely exacerbated it. We need to speak openly and honestly about this problem. That does not mean that you need to publicly confess your sin, but you should address the pornography and sexual sin in the public ministry of the church while also pursuing transparency with individuals who will help you with your own struggle. If you can't do that privately with someone in your church, how can you hope to be part of the solution for not only your own struggle but for the infection spreading throughout the church around the world?

Question 6: I am a staff pastor/parachurch ministry employee/unpaid elder who struggles with pornography. No one in my congregation/parachurch ministry knows about this struggle. How and to whom should I confess this sin/go for help?

Go first to somebody in leadership (the lead pastor if that is not you) and also to somebody with whom you have a strong relationship. Those two realities may reside in the same person, but if they don't, you need to have this conversation with multiple people. It is essential that someone in leadership knows about the struggle because they are charged with the care of all the sheep in the flock. That means they need to know about potential threats to the local body—which includes your struggle with porn. That person is also going to hold you accountable personally and professionally. Having a strong relationship with someone in the church to whom you are personally accountable is necessary, because that relationship's ground is already broken up, plowed, and prepared for growth and flourishing. You already know he loves you and you love him. This will make it easier for you to be honest, real, and raw with him. It also increases the likelihood that he will demonstrate true Christlike love, grace, and mercy toward you and lovingly confront you when necessary.

Question 7: I am a pastor/elder and another pastor at my church or in my sphere of influence has recently confessed pornography use. What early steps do I need to take in this situation?

First of all, thank God that he has led this brother to share with you. Second, encourage your brother that he has made a significant step toward repentance and growth in Christ. Affirm your love and appreciation for him. Acknowledge the courage it took to come to you and confess this sin. Through this and your continued love and friendship, you are putting flesh to the grace, mercy, and love of Christ described in the Scriptures. After you have done these things, your next steps will depend on your relationship to one another and the roles that you play in your local church contexts. If you are in separate churches, you will want to encourage him to confess his sin to another leader in his congregation. You can use the answers in this book to point out the need and value of immediate accountability in the local church. You can also offer to accompany him for this conversation and commit to being an additional relationship for external accountability if that is wise for you and him.

If you both serve on staff at the same church, your next steps (after the first two mentioned above) will depend on your roles in the church and whether or not your church has policies in place that offer guidance for this situation. If there are policies in place, follow them. Whether or not you agree with them, trying to change them in the midst of a disclosure is not wise.

If there aren't policies in place to follow and you are the lead pastor, we would encourage you to prayerfully begin the counseling process with this man and his wife (if he is married). You can use this book and its companion as guides to walk through the process. You will need to do some initial investigation to determine the level of struggle, the commitment to change, and whether or not removal from ministry is going to be necessary at this time. If removal is not indicated, then recruit a counseling ally or ally couple and begin working with this pastor to foster resolute repentance in his life.

If there are no policies and you are not the lead pastor, then you need to encourage the other pastor to confess to the lead pastor. Again, encourage him by accompanying him to the conversation (if he desires) and being willing to walk alongside him through this process and beyond.

Question 8: What should ongoing accountability look like for a pastor/ elder/ministry leader who struggles with pornography?

Ongoing accountability for a ministry leader is going to involve the same elements of accountability discussed throughout this book with a couple of additional measures. First, someone else who is a leader in the church must be a part of the accountability relationship. This is not essential for all church members, but it is for a leader.

A level of professional accountability must be in place for staff pastors/ministry leaders. A ministry leader's vocation can be at risk when he is struggling with pornography. Because of this he should not be left to himself to make the decision about his qualification for this role. At least one other person who is in a position of professional authority (able to take action to remove him if necessary) needs to be aware of his struggle and (at the least) maintain an active awareness of the accountability process. This can be a senior pastor if the individual is on staff with multiple pastors, an elder or member of the ruling board if he is the lead or solo pastor, or a member of the board of directors for parachurch ministry leaders.

Additionally, because of the often-transient nature of ministry jobs, pastors and ministry leaders who struggle with sexual temptation need external accountability from strong believers who know them well and are committed, lifetime friends. Often another minister who serves in a similar ministry will be a great ally. If the pastor is married, his wife should also be apprised of both of these relationships and be able to call on them at any time.

Question 9: How should I weigh the risk to our livelihood since a confession of pornography use may cost me my ministry job?

The question you are asking is an important one. You are in a scary situation. Your concern that you will potentially face disciplinary measures at work is reasonable, and it comes with a common temptation to ignore or even cover up blatant sexual sin because bringing it to light will put your family's reputation and livelihood on the line. Many pastors and ministry leaders have been fired for porn use (and other forms of sexual sin). Uncovering your sin, then awaiting whatever consequences may come, will be painful and stressful, but you aren't alone. God will be with you every step of the way, and others have walked this path of brave obedience. As you seek to honor God, he will sustain you. God will provide for you. There are far more valuable things at risk than a job or, even, your home. Your soul could be on the line. If you continue to hide your sin and refuse to repent, this is potential evidence that you lack saving faith. Ask yourself which is ultimately better—to lose my most valuable material possessions and gain victory over the sin that wants to eat me alive or to keep my bank account balance steady and give sin an opportunity to master me (Matthew 16:24-27)? Eternity is long; this life is short.

Question 10: I feel like I am living a lie. How should I deal with feelings of hypocrisy while I continue to serve in a ministry setting and fight an ongoing battle against porn?

Our question is why do you feel like you are living a lie? It's possible that you feel like you are living a lie because you are living a lie. Does anyone in your church, parachurch ministry, community group, circle of Christian friends, or extended family know about your struggle with porn? If the answer is no, then your feelings are correct. You are living a lie. One of the greatest gifts that accountability bestows upon the one who comes confessing sin is the comfort of being known. Psalm 139:1–12 reminds us that we can't go anywhere and be hidden from the gaze of God. He knows and sees us. That's one thing that makes the gospel so glorious. God came for us with full knowledge of who we are and what we've done. God always truly knows us, and he still has bountiful compassion. So much that he sent Jesus to die for our sins because he knew our plight. We can't accept Jesus until we are willing to admit that we are sinners. It shouldn't come as a great surprise to your Christian friends when you confess sin to them. They are sinners too, and they have already recognized sin within themselves and admitted that to God. The church should be the first place where people feel comfortable admitting the specifics of their sins. This isn't always the case, and the church needs to ask, how have we created an environment where people don't feel that they can be honest about their struggles? Could it be that you need to lead by example? Perhaps if you start by confessing your sexual sin to a few people at your church who can offer you care and accountability, this may be the catalyst for making your church a shelter for repentant souls. What if your church comes to be known as a place that is marked by consistent repentance, rather than hypocrisy? If that sounds appealing, you need to set a good example. Take the lead in making it such a place by consistently repenting and seeking out accountability for yourself.

Maybe in the past you confessed your sin to God, people in spiritual authority over you, your spouse, and one or two accountability partners, yet you still feel like a hypocrite. Do you continue to have ongoing, honest conversation with those same people about your struggle with sexual sin? Are you hiding sins from them currently and/or now refusing to confess to God? If you are maintaining each of these relationships with honesty, real-time confession, and repentance, then there aren't sin skeletons in your closet. In this case you are not a hypocrite. Everyone in your life does not need to know about all your sin struggles in order for you to avoid the label of hypocrite. People who are part of the solution need to be aware of the problem, not everyone else. You are forgiven and loved by God. Your friends also truly know you and they love you too. Ask God to use your mistakes for good. He can do that. Look for ways to use vulnerability and authenticity to bless others, even if it creates discomfort for you. Jesus set aside comfort for the good of the church. Let him be your best example as you try to do the same.

It is also common for people in ministry to feel like hypocrites when there is a significant gap between what we teach and how we sometimes live. This is true for every human being who walks on this earth. As a minister of the gospel and a teacher of God's Word, there will be times when our teaching does not match our lives. This is not hypocrisy. Claiming we have no sin or that we are in full compliance with God's law is hypocrisy. God's law is perfect. The standard of obedience for having a relationship with him is perfection. The Scriptures are given to us, in part, to show us the gap between our lives and his holiness. But they are also given to point us to the only one who could bridge that gap and bring us into relationship with God through our Savior, Jesus Christ. So when you begin to feel like a hypocrite, examine yourself with the questions above, make adjustments where necessary, and in all of these scenarios remember Christ. Remember the gospel. Remember salvation comes by grace alone, through faith alone, in Christ alone (Ephesians 2:8-9, Titus 3:5).

Appendix 3

Is Pornography Use Grounds for Divorce?

BEFORE I ANSWER the question of whether or not pornography use is grounds for divorce, I want to encourage you to pursue marriage counseling with a biblical counselor if divorce has been brought up by either you or your wife. Divorce is no small matter. If either of you is contemplating divorce, or if the threat of divorce has been thrown around in your fights, you need to seek marriage counseling with a biblical counselor as soon as possible.

To a serious degree, porn use violates the exclusivity of the marriage covenant. It is a form of sexual immorality. At the same time, porn use is something less than an adulterous relationship because it lacks physical or emotional connection to another person. There's a spectrum of sexual sin that moves from lustful thoughts to adulterous relationships. Pornography use lands somewhere between those two sins. This does not mean you can have porn and your wife both without relational or spiritual repercussions. Sexual sin is insidious and infectious. If you struggle with porn and are unrepentant, porn will eventually master you. In time you may outgrow these visually oriented cravings and seek increasingly brazen forms of sexual expression to fulfill your longings. Porn unconfessed doesn't relent or lead solely to a little more porn—it often leads to violent porn, child porn, sexting someone from work, online sexual chats with strangers, strip clubs, prostitutes, and affairs. Those things are all grounds for separation and potentially lead to divorce. If you have not yet exhibited repentance, but also haven't ventured down any of these increasingly deviant roads, praise God that he has thus far kept you from greater destruction. Then seek out accountability without delay and commit to ongoing transparency in your local church, so they can pray for you and support you as you pursue godly transformation. God is the only One who can change your heart.

In short, Jenny and I believe that a spouse viewing pornography it is not grounds for divorce because it is not the same as adultery. To show you why we have come to this conclusion, we will deconstruct the typical arguments used to support the idea that pornography use is an offense for which divorce is an acceptable end to the marriage. Looking at several different passages in the Bible that focus on Jesus's teaching regarding divorce and adultery, most people agree that adultery is grounds for divorce (Deuteronomy 24:1–4; Matthew 19:3–12; Mark 10:1–12; Luke 16:18). In Matthew 5:27–28, Jesus says, "You have heard that it was said, 'You shall not commit adultery.' But I say to you that everyone who looks at a woman with lustful intent has already committed adultery with her in his heart." As the argument goes, this makes lust (clearly including pornography) equal to adultery and therefore a divorceable offense.

Let's put this argument into a logical syllogism:

Adultery is a divorceable offense.

Pornography use is adultery.

Therefore, pornography use is a divorceable offense.

The problem lies in the second premise. This idea that pornography use is identical to adultery is faulty. Jesus does not say that lust and the act of adultery are identical sins and thus incur the same human/legal consequences.

We can see the problem with the logic if we place Matthew 5:27–28 back into its context. Just prior to this, Jesus uses the same argument demonstrating the connection between murder and anger/hatred. In verses 21–22, Jesus says, "You have heard that it was said to those of old, 'You shall not murder; and whoever murders will be liable to judgment.' But I say to you that everyone who is angry with his brother will be liable to judgment; whoever insults his brother will be liable to the council; and whoever says, 'You fool!' will be liable to the hell of fire." Applying the same logic as was used above, we see this syllogism:

> Murder is a legally punishable offense (jail or
> death penalty).
> Anger is murder.
> Therefore, anger is legally punishable with jail time
> or death.

Obviously, no one wants to start applying that text in this fashion. Our jails (and death row) would be overflowing with inmates, and we would all be among those serving sentences.

We do not intend to undermine the seriousness of pornography; as we stated before, pornography use is a heinous sin, and we want to fight it. However, in this passage, Jesus was not trying to make literal statements about the legal consequences of sin; he was elevating people's awareness of the seriousness of sin and conveying that it is not merely how we act externally that matters. We don't need only externally constrained behavior; we need internally transformed hearts.

Another argument sometimes used to declare pornography as a divorceable offense is rooted in the vocabulary Jesus uses in Matthew 5:32 and 19:3–9. When the Pharisees question Jesus on the lawfulness of a man divorcing his wife, Jesus first establishes the high value God places on marriage by stating, "Have you not read that he who created them from the beginning made them male and female, and said, 'Therefore a man shall leave his father and his mother and hold fast to his wife, and the two shall become one flesh'? So they are no longer two, but one flesh. What therefore God has joined together, let not man separate" (Matthew 19:4–6). When they press him on the question by pointing out the fact that Moses allowed men to divorce their wives (Deuteronomy 24:1–4) Jesus responds, "Because of your hardness of heart Moses allowed you to divorce your wives, but from the beginning it was not so. And I say to you: whoever divorces his wife, except for sexual immorality, and marries another, commits adultery" (Matthew 19:8–9). In these verses Jesus uses two terms to describe sexual sin: *moicheia*, which is translated "adultery," and *porneia*, which is "sexual immorality." In normal usage, *moicheia* refers to sexual activity by a married person with someone besides his/her spouse.[1] *Porneia*, on the other hand, is a term with a broader semantic domain, including other forms of sexual sin such as prostitution, unchastity, and fornication.[2]

The logic flowing from the argument is this: If one divorces for something other than *porneia*, then they commit adultery (*moicheia*); therefore, divorcing for *porneia* is allowed. Accepting this line of reason, we must answer the question, Does pornography use qualify as *porneia*? And we must consider the following points to answer this question.

First, just because we get the word *pornography* from the word *porneia* does not mean that pornography necessarily qualifies as *porneia*. This is a common misstep people fall into when they do word studies as part of their Bible study. One example of this is when preachers say that God has "explosive power" because the word *dynamite* comes from the word *dunamis*, which is translated as "power" in the New Testament (92 times in the English Standard Version). They are reading dynamite back into *dunamis*, but dynamite was not invented until hundreds of years after the New Testament was written.[3] Likewise, although *porneia* is the root word for what we call pornography today, it neither affirms nor denies that modern porn equals *porneia*. The etymology of pornography cannot be the only grounds by which we determine whether or not it qualifies as *porneia*.

Second, Jesus's response to the Pharisees leans toward a narrower limitation on divorce, not a more expansive position. We need to keep this in mind with any discussion of divorce and be on guard for people who seem to be rushing to divorce or approaching it with a flippant attitude.

Third, the term *porneia*, while including more sexual deviancy than only adultery, still describes sexual acts with another human being. Pornography that doesn't spill over into sexual activity with other people is more in line with what Jesus addressed in Matthew 5:27–28, which we discussed above.

Fourth, certain extreme cases of pornography use may come within the parameters of a divorceable offense. The case has been made that where pornography and masturbation has completely supplanted the sexual activity between a husband and wife, it violates the one-flesh relationship of marriage and therefore qualifies as adultery.[4]

Finally, as we mentioned above, unfettered, unaddressed, unrepentant pornography use will tend to spiral into worse sin, often turning into illicit sexual activity involving other people. Some types of pornography and inappropriate sexual behavior within marriage are illegal and bring with them legal consequences and potentially divorce, including child-pornography, marital rape, sexual abuse in marriage, etc. Our encouragement to you is to allow others in your church, hopefully your biblical counselor, pastor, and other spiritual leaders, to help you make any decision regarding the ending of marriage. It is a difficult decision with weighty consequences that should not be entered into lightly. Invite others into the process of making that decision with you.

Remember, just because divorce is permissible does not mean it is mandatory. There are many people who pursue forgiveness and reconciliation even in instances of adultery. However, there are times when divorce is appropriate. We cannot outline each and every scenario here, nor can we speak directly to your individual situation, so please reach out for help and wisdom from people near you who know you.

Endnotes

Chapter 1

1. Isabelle Senechal, "A Story of Survivors and Statistics: Fighting the Scandal of Human Trafficking," *America* 222, no. 14 (June 22, 2020): 28–33; Allison J. Luzwick, "Human Trafficking and Pornography: Using the Trafficking Victims Protection Act to Prosecute Trafficking for the Production of Internet Pornography," *Northwestern University Law Review* 112, no. 2 (March 2017): 355–75.

2. Patrick F. Fagan, "The Effects of Pornography on Individuals, Marriage, Family, and Community," *Marri Research Synthesis*, December 2009, https://downloads.frc.org/EF/EF12D43.pdf; Donald L. Hilton and Clark Watts, "Pornography Addiction: A Neuroscience Perspective," *Surgical Neurology International* 2 (February 21, 2011): 19.

3. Fagan, "The Effects of Pornography on Individuals, Marriage, Family, and Community"; Jennifer P. Schneider, "Effects of Cybersex Addiction on the Family: Results of a Survey," *Sexual Addiction & Compulsivity* 7, no. 1/2 (January 2000): 31–58.8,9. A brief survey was completed by 91 women and 3 men, aged 24-57, who had experienced serious adverse consequences of their partner's cybersex involvement. In 60.6% of cases the sexual activities were limited to cybersex and did not include offline sex. Although not specifically asked about this, 31% of partners volunteered that the cybersex activities were a continuation of preexisting compulsive sexual behaviors. Open-ended questions yielded the following conclusions: 1. In response to learning about their partner's online sexual activities, the survey respondents felt hurt, betrayal, rejection, abandonment, devastation, loneliness, shame, isolation,

humiliation, jealousy, and anger, as well as loss of self-esteem. Being lied to repeatedly was a major cause of distress. 2. Cybersex addiction was a major contributing factor to separation and divorce of couples in this survey: 22.3% of the respondents were separated or divorced, and several others were seriously contemplating leaving. 3. Among 68% of the couples one or both had lost interest in relational sex: 52.1% of addicts had decreased interest in sex with their spouse, as did 34% of partners. Some couples had no relational sex in months or years. 4. Partners compared themselves unfavorably with the online women (or men).

4. Fagan, "The Effects of Pornography on Individuals, Marriage, Family, and Community."

Chapter 2

1. Robert W. Kellemen, *God's Healing for Life's Losses: How to Find Hope When You're Hurting* (Winona Lake, IN: BMH Books, 2010), 21.

2. Mark Vroegop, *Dark Clouds, Deep Mercy: Discovering the Grace of Lament* (Wheaton, IL: Crossway, 2019), 30; Kellemen, *God's Healing for Life's Losses*, 31–36.

3. Vroegop, *Dark Clouds, Deep Mercy*, 21.

4. Vroegop, *Dark Clouds, Deep Mercy*, 26.

5. Kellemen, *God's Healing for Life's Losses*, 16.

Chapter 3

1. Horst Robert Balz and Gerhard Schneider, *Exegetical Dictionary of the New Testament,* vol. 2 (Grand Rapids, MI: Eerdmans, 1990), 41.

2. L. Berkhof, *Systematic Theology* (Grand Rapids, MI: Eerdmans, 1938), 487.

Chapter 4

1. L. Berkhof, *Systematic Theology* (Grand Rapids, MI: Eerdmans, 1938), 487.

2. Gerhard Kittel, Gerhard Friedrich, and Geoffrey William Bromiley, eds., *Theological Dictionary of the New Testament* (Grand Rapids, MI: Eerdmans, 1985), 687.

Chapter 5

1. David Powlison, *Good and Angry: Redeeming Anger, Irritation, Complaining, and Bitterness* (Greensboro, NC: New Growth Press, 2016), 80–87.

Chapter 7

1. Mightyoaksprograms.org
2. Ron, DeHass, "What Are the Most Up-to-Date Stats on Pornography?" Covenant Eyes, accessed August 9, 2021, https://www.covenant eyes.com/pornstats/.

Chapter 8

1. Joyce Baldwin, *1 And 2 Samuel: An Introduction and Commentary*, vol. 8, Tyndale Old Testament Commentaries (Downers Grove: InterVarsity Press, 1989), 158.
2. James Swanson, *Dictionary of Biblical Languages with Semantic Domains: Hebrew (Old Testament)* (Oak Harbor: Logos Research Systems, 2002).

Appendix 1

1. Special thanks to Chris Moles who encouraged me to add this appendix and helped me with the content.
2. These are adapted from the "Warning Signs Quiz" at https://www.calledtopeace.org/resources/warning-signs-quiz/.

Appendix 2

1. Robert W. Yarbrough, *The Letters to Timothy and Titus*, The Pillar New Testament Commentary (Grand Rapids, MI: Eerdmans, 2018), 479.

Appendix 3

1. Kittel, Friedrich, and Bromiley, *Theological Dictionary of the New Testament*, 606.
2. Kittel, Friedrich, and Bromiley, 918; Frederick W. Danker, Walter Bauer, and William Arndt, *A Greek-English Lexicon of the New Testament and Other Early Christian Literature*, 3rd ed. (Chicago: University of Chicago Press, 2000), 854.
3. D. A. Carson, *Exegetical Fallacies*, 2nd ed. (Grand Rapids: Baker Books, 1996), 33–35.
4. John M. Frame, *The Doctrine of the Christian Life*, A Theology of Lordship (Phillipsburg, NJ: P & R Publishing, 2008), 774–76; Jim Newheiser, *Marriage, Divorce, and Remarriage: Critical Questions and Answers* (Phillipsburg: P&R Publishing, 2017), 240–42.